Austin –
Best wishes for
many successes

Jerry Elmore

THE 5 BEST PRACTICES OF HIGHLY EFFECTIVE SALES MANAGERS

A GUIDE TO LEADING HIGH PERFORMANCE SALES TEAMS

BY JERRY D. ELMORE

authorHOUSE™

1663 LIBERTY DRIVE, SUITE 200
BLOOMINGTON, INDIANA 47403
(800) 839-8640
WWW.AUTHORHOUSE.COM

First published by AuthorHouse 03/18/05

ISBN: 1-4208-3165-8 (sc)
ISBN: 1-4208-3164-X (dj)

Library of Congress Control Number: 2005901370

Printed in the United States of America
Bloomington, Indiana

This book is printed on acid-free paper.

dedication

Dedicated in memory of Mathew B. McCormick, a highly effective Sales Manager

acknowledgments

Everything I know about being a highly effective sales manager I have learned from someone else. My first real "aha" experience came when I got my first sales manager job and realized that I didn't know how to be one! Even though I had worked under one very good sales manager, and I thought I knew how to do what he did, I didn't. So, I went to St. Louis, MO and attended Psychological Associates, Inc.'s Dimensional Sales Management Training. Later I attended the Leadership Effectiveness Training program by Dr. Thomas Gordon. I will be forever thankful for the insights and skills these two programs provided me as I developed The Five Best Practices.

Throughout my sales management career, I worked with many sales managers who were my peers in other regions. Thank you for your help and insights.

Thank you to the many sales executives who have given their feedback after attending my training sessions.

As I wrote this book, there were many sales executives that read the manuscript and gave me their input. A special thanks to: Charlie Kettle, CEO, First Commercial Bank, Huntsville, AL; Steve Olson, President, Generative Consulting, Atlanta, GA; Bob Robbins, Senior Vice President, Synovus Insurance Services; Catherine Storey, Regional Sales Manager, Synovus Financial Corp; Wendy Northington, Vice President Sales, Marketing, and Product Development, Synovus Financial Corp.

Two of my sons who are in sales, Kevin Elmore and Michael Elmore reviewed the manuscript and gave me input. Thanks to both of you.

Thanks to Dan Hubley and the folks at Bluefish Bay Editing and Publishing Services for providing the editing expertise.

Finally, a special thanks to my wife Nina. Her support, encouragement, input and suggestions kept me going. Hon, you're the best!

Contents

sales manager

The Bridge to High Performance Sales
Introduction

The subtitle of this book is *A Guide to Leading High Performance Sales Teams*. It is a guidebook and a reference book for new as well as experienced sales managers who want to optimize the selling efforts of their salespeople to achieve the desired levels of sales volume, profits, and growth necessary for a thriving organization. It focuses on five critical best practices that, when used consistently and systematically, result in highly effective and efficient sales teams. It doesn't cover topics like interviewing, hiring, compensation, forecasting, or sales force automation, although these things are all important. (The appendix will list books that will help the sales manager in those and other areas.) This book is for the sales manager who finds him/herself in the same position I found myself when I got my first sales manager position: an existing sales team leader who needed to tap the full potential of each salesperson on my team.

When I made the transition from salesperson to sales manager thirty years ago, although I needed to learn how to create job descriptions, interview, and hire prospective salespeople, structure compensation plans, forecast, and myriad other tasks, my immediate need was, "How do I move my sales team from where they are to where they need to be? How do I improve the performance of the stars as well as the non-stars, using methods that motivate both?" I quickly found that managing was one part of the equation, but leadership was an equal and oftentimes more important issue if I were to develop my people to become all that they could be. This book shows sales managers how to be the bridge to develop salespeople individually and develop the individuals into highly effective and efficient sales teams.

The Importance of Developing Salespeople

Developing salespeople is not the role that many sales managers thought they were taking on when they got the job of sales manager. How important is the development role for a sales manager? In a study done by The Forum Corporation, a Boston-based training and consulting firm, Jocelyn Davis, Vice President of Product Development, quoted a survey they had done:

> "All of our respondents were unanimous in saying the most important role for sales managers today—and also the role they

need the most help with—is the coaching and developing of their sales staff." [1]

As the survey respondents showed and as I have experienced, the role sales managers need the most help with is coaching and developing their sales staff. Coaching and developing salespeople is as much leadership as it is management. To coach and develop others takes a coach's attitude, which we will look at in Chapter 1. Chapters 2 through 6 focus on the five best practices of highly effective sales managers that enable them to develop and create consistently high performing sales teams. These best practices are:

1. Define and clearly communicate expectations

2. Observe sales team's use of the critical selling activities

3. Assess strengths and areas for development

4. Coach individually and as a team for optimum performance

5. Hold salespeople accountable

These five best practices constitute a process highly effective sales managers' use that has a substantial, immediate impact on the sales productivity of every salesperson; the stars as well as the non-stars. Salesperson development is the focal point of these five best practices. By using the process consistently and systematically, a discipline is developed, which sustains long-term sales results. Webster's College Dictionary defines "process" as "a continuing development involving

---

[1]"What Makes An Ideal Sales Manager?" *Selling Power Magazine;* (June 2001) Reprinted by permission..

many changes; a method of doing something, with all the steps." This definition accurately explains what effective sales managers do to develop their sales teams' selling abilities. Sales managers cause continuing development through change. Robert J. Calvin, in his book *Sales Management*[2], says:

> "The best sales managers realize they are agents of change and, as such they must manage change and change people's behavior . . . (they) have what I like to call the will to manage. They are willing to set standards, be critical, and sit in judgment. (They) don't whine about their salespeople. They work to change their behavior through non-monetary motivation."

What results can we expect from sales managers who accomplish the necessary changes? Calvin goes on to say:

"Good sales management, properly applied, is the least expensive, most effective way to increase dollars of revenue and margins, market share, cash flow, return on investment, and net present value, as well as to beat the competition and make yourself a hero."[2]

Developing Salespeople Is a Challenging Task

Developing salespeople is truly a challenging task for sales managers. Most sales managers come from the ranks of highly effective salespeople where their only responsibility was their own efforts. They were excellent producers of sales. As producers they were measured by their personal

---

[2]. Reprinted by permission of McGraw-Hill Companies, Robert J. Calvin, SALESMANAGEMENT Copyright© 2001

production. But once they step into the ranks of sales management, the focus changes. Sales managers are no longer producers (although some have revenue generating responsibilities) measured by their own selling success. Sales managers are now measured by the success of others, something they're not used to. Being a sales manager is about providing the opportunity to help others grow—professionally and personally—to develop others, not about your own personal production.

Why Use the Five Best Practices?

Why use these five best practices? Because every sales team has at least two categories of sales talent: those who are outstanding performers and those who make up the balance. The outstanding performers are often referred to as "natural born salespeople." Every time I hear someone called a natural born salesperson, I remember what Zig Ziglar, the motivational speaker, said about natural born salespeople. He said that he had traveled all over the world and had seen announcements where women gave birth to boys and women give birth to girls. But he'd never seen an announcement where a woman gave birth to a "salesperson." Yet he read in newspapers where salespeople die, so something had to happen between birth and death. Of course, what happens is that salespeople are developed, not born. And the most effective way to develop people, both stars and non-stars, is by using a process consistently and systematically. Therefore, each salesperson has the potential to be the best they can be, even if they are not born with those so-called "natural" characteristics.

The Five Best Practices Develops Individuals and Teams

Not only does using the five best practices develop individuals, it develops the entire team. How important is it to develop the entire team? A story is told that exemplifies the importance of the entire team. In 1986 the Penn State University football team played Boston College, who had the Heisman Trophy winner Doug Flutie on their team but the Penn State team won that game. Penn State played the University of Georgia when Hershel Walker was the Heisman Trophy winner and, again, Penn State won that game. Penn State played the University of Southern California when Marcus Allen was the Heisman Trophy winner. Penn State won the game. Even though Boston College, University of Southern California, and University of Georgia had an outstanding individual and athlete, the point is that the Penn State team won the games. No matter whether we have a star performer on our sales team, the team functions better when it functions as a team. Sales managers who follow the five best practices build high performing individuals and high performance sales teams.

We'll look at how the practices enable Sales managers to build high performing individuals and teams throughout the remainder of this book. But first, starting in the next chapter, we will look at the core competency that is a key to all highly effective Sales managers: attitude of a coach.

chapter one

Attitude of a Coach

Did anyone ever say to you, "You've got an attitude"? Usually when anyone talks about someone having an "attitude," the connotation is negative. But everyone has an attitude and it's not always negative. Attitude is a mental disposition that governs the way we express ourselves and the way we present ourselves. You've seen the person who is a domineering type individual, has a definite opinion on everything, and is quick to express it. She "tells it like it is" and the "way it is" is the way *she* sees it. Or, you may have witnessed the person who is reticent, mostly quiet, is slow to accept things, is cautious, and not very vocal. He might even be thought of as stubborn because he seems only interested in following the status quo. Then there's the person who never met a stranger, loves everyone, and wants everyone to love her. She always focuses on pleasant things, never on anything that could cause confrontation. And finally, there's the person who is decisive and challenging, who has high standards, is assertive but not aggressive, and is bottom-line oriented.

Attitude Impacts Others

Each of the attitudes mentioned above have an impact on the sales staff. But which attitude has the most positive impact, the impact that a highly effective sales manager would want to have? Let me tell you about my experience with sales managers who have had one of the aforementioned attitudes. You may recognize yourself or someone you have worked with in my examples.

The Critic

My first sales manager was a fellow I'll call Herb. Herb had an MBA, and had been very successful in sales with the company. He had been promoted to sales manager after only a short time with the company because he had been so successful. Herb's communication style was "he talked and you listened." He let me know right away that there was one way to do things: Herb's way. If I did that, we would get along fine. If not, there were plenty of salespeople looking for jobs and the underlying message was that I could be replaced. Herb never seemed to have a kind or positive word to say; if you asked me, I would have told you that he couldn't have cared less about me and what I needed.

When Herb traveled with me, he took over. It was important, he said, for me to see how it ought to be done. And, of course, the way it ought to be done was Herb's way. Herb couldn't let go and let me take over. It was too painful for him to see someone not do it his way. Herb was very excitable, especially when a customer would say, "I'm not interested" or "No." In fact, Herb believed that the sale began when the customer said, "No." (That was the title of a sales book Herb used to quote). I believe that some people bought from us just to get us out of their office. And yes, we did get thrown out of some places, but that didn't deter Herb. He always blamed it on the fact that I hadn't set up a good prospect.

When we looked at my results, which we did on a regular basis, we didn't spend any time on what I was doing right and what I might do differently. We spent time talking about what wasn't happening, nothing about what was happening. Our sales meetings were lectures where Herb stressed what wasn't happening and how we would have to work harder to make our numbers. Interestingly, I was somewhat successful with Herb as my sales manager, because I was afraid not to be! I didn't learn much from Herb because, although at first I tried to do things the way he told me, I found that that just wasn't me. So I was very uncomfortable when we were together.

What was the impact of Herb's attitude? He did get short-term results because like me, everyone on the sales team was afraid not to produce! During my tenure with Herb, I noticed there was high turnover; we were constantly losing good salespeople and having to replace them. Morale was low; complaining and excuse making by the sales staff was common. There were instances when some of the salespeople actually did exactly what Herb told them to do, often resulting in disastrous results since there should have been an alternative method used. Herb had the attitude of a critic, not the attitude of a coach.

The Fatalist

A second sales manager I had I'll call Bert. Other than the goals the company handed down to Bert, which he passed along to us, I couldn't tell you what he expected of me. He didn't seem to care what I did or how I did it, so long as I produced and followed the company policies. Bert's attitude was that they had hired an experienced salesperson so there was no need for any sales management. His assumption was that if you find the right person, you don't need to train them to sell or manage the sales effort once they're on board.

Bert never traveled with me in the three years I was with this company, never saw me with a customer, and never gave me any coaching. After my experience with Herb, that suited me fine. He sent me monthly reports on my progress to quota, but we never talked about them. Once in awhile there would be a penciled note from Bert on the report showing some area that was deficient, but nothing else.

At sales meetings Bert focused on product knowledge, company policies and procedures, and what upper management wanted done. Although product knowledge is very important in selling, it is only one element in the selling process. Developing trust and determining needs is far more significant in selling than product knowledge. Many salespeople have an adequate understanding of their product, but fail to build the trust and determine the needs of the prospect to get an opportunity to deliver a solution. If all that was needed was product knowledge to become the best salesperson, then computer programmers would definitely be the best salespeople for computer systems and auto mechanics would be the best salespeople for cars. However, most computer programmers and auto mechanics do not make the best salespeople. Being able to build rapport and trust, being able to analyze a prospect's problems and getting buy-in that action needs to be taken, and then showing how the product or service will provide value to the prospect is what successful professional salespeople do. Product knowledge is only a small part of this process. In Bert's sales meetings, we never got beyond just the facts, data, and statistics, which are not enough to make winning salespeople.

During my time working with Bert, I noticed that there was a lot of indifference among the sales staff, a kind of "whatever" attitude. There was little passion, which is interesting among a sales group, since sales types tend to be pretty passionate. We didn't have a lot of turnover, but from what I saw, we needed to have some. Undesirable performance was seldom punished, and desirable performance was seldom recognized. Productivity per salesperson was adequate, but just adequate. Performance could have been considerably better. There was a lot of wasted time on insignificant tasks, things I would call paper shuffling. But Bert didn't get involved. He seemed to be one of those people who have the attitude, "It won't help anyway, so why try? You can't get people to do something they don't want to do." Bert had the attitude of a fatalist, not the attitude of a coach.

The Cheerleader

At my third sales position, I'll call my sales manager Phil. Everyone loved Phil and Phil loved everyone. In fact, that's one of the reasons I was interested in working for him. He was such a great guy. And after working with Bert and Herb, Phil seemed like a breath of fresh air. Although he loved to visit and talk, the only thing Phil communicated to me about goals was that they were very broad and could be revised if need be.

When Phil traveled with me, and he loved to travel with the sales staff, he was always positive. I can't ever remember hearing him say one negative thing. He never confronted me about anything even though there were some times I felt confrontation would have been the right action. No matter what I did, either it just wasn't discussed or it received a hearty, "Good job!" When I'd get my monthly reports, Phil would compliment me on the areas I did well, and on those areas that weren't where they needed to be, he'd say, "You'll get it there. Just keep at it." Sales meetings were long, filled with rambling talk about sports, family, and what a great job we all were doing, but nothing that was useful to the selling experience.

It was interesting to note, as I worked for Phil, that eventually the entire sales team and I drifted into a state of lethargy. It was comfortable and we all enjoyed working with Phil, but we weren't meeting our goals. Even if I went to Phil for sales advice, I didn't get it. He didn't want to try to tell someone how to do something for fear of seeming negative or causing confrontation. Phil had the attitude of a cheerleader, which we sometimes needed but not all the time. Although I liked Phil a lot, just like everyone else, I soon found that I wasn't growing and neither were my sales. So I moved on.

The Coach

At my fourth sales position, a man I'll call Nat was my sales manager. Nat was active and decisive; he had a warm but challenging attitude. I felt that he was interested in me as a person and wanted to see me excel. Although Nat could be really tough at times, he was always fair. At first I was a little reluctant to take this job, because Nat was very clear about how his team worked. He very clearly communicated his expectations. Although he had revenue responsibilities himself, he spent time with me in my territory making calls and observing me using my selling skills; not so he could criticize me afterward, but so that we could determine what I was doing well and what I needed to do differently. And even though I had a lot of experience and had been moderately successful, Nat showed me how I could improve. Results were important, and we assessed those results so that I could learn from them.

Nat believed in one-on-one coaching; he helped me develop my latent abilities and optimize my performance. We met weekly to discuss what I had done last week and the results I accomplished, and we talked about next week's plans and goals that I had set. We always had goals, and we reviewed them weekly. Each month, Nat made sure that we all had an opportunity in our sales meetings to focus on a specific selling skill that wasn't quite where it needed to be. Given my experience with

Herb, Bert and Phil, I was at times a little taken-aback to have such a hands-on sales manager. But Nat's focus was on my growth and it paid off in my productivity. I always felt, even though I didn't always like it, that he was interested in making me the best I could be. That sounded pretty good to me. Although I had been successful in my previous sales positions, while working with Nat I reached heights I never imagined possible. By the end of three years I had tripled the number of accounts in the territory, was the second highest producer in the office of five salespeople, and had tripled my income.

Motivate Others to Be All They Can Be

What did I learn from working with Nat? Here was a person who was interested in developing his people. Although he was results-focused, he worked to help those who were not performing to improve and motivated those that were to perform even better. Nat gave us a great deal of autonomy, allowing us to have experiences that enabled us to grow. He enabled us to "be all that we could be." Some of the sales staff didn't want to "be all they could be" and they left the team voluntarily. Others left at Nat's request. Nat dealt with issues as they arose even though dealing with them might be uncomfortable. He didn't deal with them in front of the team, and not in a way that destroyed the person. People were involved and growing; they produced and were committed. There was recognition and praise but only when it was deserved. Nat had the attitude of a coach.

Validating the Affects of Attitude

Is there any validation to my experience with these very different sales managers? Yes, I found out later, there is. In a study done by one life insurance company, the company grouped its sales managers into two categories: half who were most effective and half who were less effective. The company tested potential recruit's sales aptitude prior to hiring and then kept records of their results after they were trained at corporate headquarters. The recruits were then sent to work in either the effective sales managers' branches or the less effective sales managers' branches. Forty-eight percent of those recruits who had the highest sales aptitude scores and were sent to work with the effective sales managers became successful, while only 27 percent of those with the same high sales aptitude scores who were sent to work for the less effective sales managers became effective. Of those recruits who scored lower in sales aptitude but were hired anyway, 27 percent became successful under the most effective sales managers and only 6 percent under the less effective sales managers. The conclusion of this study is that sales management has as much to do with the success of the salesperson as the innate aptitude of the salesperson.

In another study a District Sales manager reorganized his sales managers into three groups: those he considered his best managers, those he considered average, and those he considered his least able managers. Next, he placed his best salespeople with the best managers, the next-best salespeople with the average manager, and his low producers with the manager he considered his least able manager. The best salespeople increased their sales; the low producers produced less than they had before the change. And, more of the low producers quit their jobs. An interesting aspect to this study was the middle group. The expectation was that this group would produce average results. But the average manager took on the attitude of a coach, refusing to believe that he and his team were any less capable than the best manager and his team. He continually communicated positive expectations to his group and led them persistently with hard work. The results: they performed higher than the best salespeople. The attitude of a coach produces results!

Why Not Just Send Them to Training?

Many people have the misconception that training is all that is needed, not sales management. These people send their salespeople to a two- or three-day training session and expect that to replace any sales management. As a matter of fact, that's what happened when I worked for Bert. I felt that I needed some help so I took sales training on my own, even paying for it myself, and my sales improved. But I eventually reached a plateau that I couldn't overcome on my own, and since Bert wasn't the kind of sales manager to get involved, I couldn't get above the plateau. This example showed me something that I later learned is a fact: sending people to training events without effective modeling, coaching, and reinforcement on the job is very ineffective. Studies show that as little as eight to 12 percent of those who attend training and get no personal follow up translate the training into performance on the job. Other studies, such as the insurance study mentioned above, show that those percentages can be expanded five-fold when effective sales managers reinforce the sales process taught in class. Training plays an important role, but training can't get the job done by itself. Without regular reinforcement through modeling and coaching, training has less than satisfactory results. Sales managers willing to meet the requirement of reinforcement are the vital link in the organization's success.

Coach Is the Right Attitude

What is the attitude that makes a highly effective sales manager? It is an attitude of wanting to help people develop their skills and talents and of empowering them to do that. It is the attitude of a coach. Looking back at the sales managers discussed in this chapter, we can see five traits of a sales manager with the attitude of a coach:

1.   Gives honest, straightforward feedback focused on behaviors and activities. (We'll discuss feedback at length in Chapter 5.) Someone with the attitude of a coach gives honest, straightforward feedback about behaviors and activities that cause success and behaviors and activities that need adjustment in order to achieve success. Herb gave a lot of negative feedback focused on the person, not about behaviors and activities that needed adjustment. However, we never heard anything about how to correct them to improve our odds of achieving success. Bert focused strictly on behaviors and activities that were important to upper management, never giving individual feedback. Phil rarely talked about behaviors and activities; he was always focusing on the person by saying, "Good job" or "You did great on that one." Nat focused on behaviors and activities. He let you know when you were doing well, and he let you know when you needed to make a change. He was honest and straightforward on both counts.

2.   Encourages salespeople to grow and expand --- to be all they can be --- to optimize their abilities. Herb expected growth and expansion, but I wouldn't say that he encouraged it. It was more of an underlying threat. Bert never talked about it. Phil encouraged us, but again, it wasn't an encouragement to grow and expand. It was just encouragement for encouragement's sake. Nat expected growth and expansion, and he worked with us to enable us to grow and expand.

3.   Listens to the salesperson as a person, and not just as an employee. Hears more than the words being expressed, and; listens for feelings. As I previously said about Herb, I never felt like I was a person with him; I was a tool he was using to make his numbers. Bert was too busy listening to what upper management wanted to ever pay attention to his sales team. Phil did listen to us and heard the feelings. However, he got so caught up in the feelings that they became an impediment. He truly felt our pain, and at times it kept us from overcoming that pain. Nat listened and heard us as more than just his sales team; when we were "hurting" he heard that, but instead of letting that be an obstacle, he worked with us to help us work through it.

4.   Keeps sales staff informed. Salespeople need information, not just the numbers. Sales managers are often involved in upper level management meetings as well as client meetings. Of course, there may be some things discussed in those meetings that can't be shared, but there are many things that can be. Keeping sales staff informed is more than just sending them an e-mail, voice mail, or memo. It's talking one-on-one as well as a group; letting them know what's happening.

5.   Walks the talk. Many sales managers are good at telling people what to do, yet seem to have a different set of criteria for their own actions and behaviors. Walking the talk is about integrity and credibility. We

know how important these two traits are in the selling process; they are just as important for the sales manager. As someone once said, "People hear what we say but they see what we do, and seeing is believing." When we walk the talk we do what we expect others to do.

What If I Don't Have a Coach's Attitude?

"But," you say, "I don't have a coach's attitude. I'm afraid that I'm more like Herb, Bert, or Phil. What am I to do?" Just telling ourselves to have the attitude of a coach won't work. So how do we modify our attitude? We modify our attitude when we modify our actions. People don't change their attitude by thinking about change, they change their behavior, which results in a change in attitude. When I was involved with a large international training organization, we used to demonstrate how to do this. Let's say that you wanted to have an enthusiastic attitude. We'd get everyone to stand up, and then we'd have everyone say over and over, while jumping from one foot to the other, "Act enthusiastic and you'll be enthusiastic!" It was amazing how quickly everyone in the room took on an enthusiastic attitude. Of course, we can't get in front of our salespeople and repeat over and over the five traits above, while jumping up and down from one foot to the other. But we can develop a coach's attitude by consistently practicing the five traits and consistently using the five best practices of highly effective sales managers as shown in the following chapters:

• Defining and clearly communicating expectations.

• Spending time with salespeople observing them at work with customers and prospects, looking for what is working well and what needs developing.

• Assessing their strengths and areas for improvement, discussing these with the salesperson, and getting buy-in on a plan for development.

• Providing individual coaching sessions where the sales manager and the salesperson discuss a call or a situation with the idea of allowing that salesperson to discover strengths and areas for development.

• Holding salespeople accountable at weekly meetings where commitments are discussed.

Now that we've seen that the right attitude is necessary to become a highly effective sales manager, let's look in the next chapter at the first of the five best practices necessary to be a highly effective sales manager: define and clearly communicate expectations.

chapter two

Best practice #1: Define & Clearly Communicate Expectations

How important is it for sales managers to define and clearly communicate expectations? One of the most dramatic examples of the power of expectations is chronicled in the book, *Don't Fire Them, Fire Them Up,* by Frank Pacetta with Roger Gittines (Simon and Schuster, 1994). Frank Pacetta was the sales manager who took over the struggling northeast Ohio Xerox office with the expectation (which he clearly defined and communicated) of making it one of the top offices, not only regionally but also nationally. Within one year of taking on the sales manager responsibilities for the office, the northeast Ohio Xerox district sales office went from nearly dead last in terms of sales and revenue, to first in the 11 Ohio regions and fourth nationally of the then 65 sales districts. Of course, this feat took more than just communicating expectations. But vision (which in itself is a form of expectation) and communicating expectations top the list of Pacetta's success process.

Other examples of the importance of expectations are outlined in Thomas K. Connellan, Ph.D.'s book, *Bringing Out the Best in Others!* (Bard Press, 2003). Connellan is a former research associate and program director at the University of Michigan. He has researched and developed proven systems for achieving high performance and has been associated with GE, Dell, Marriott, the Air Force Academy, Pacific Life, and Neiman Marcus. Connellan shows in his book that there are three keys necessary for tapping the full potential of those you manage and lead. And the first key is positive expectations. Connellan's book discusses how to improve sales, strengthen teamwork, and increase productivity using the three keys. He makes the point that the expectations of those in charge have a significant impact on the performance of others.

The Purpose of Communicating Expectations

The purpose of communicating expectations is to ensure that the sales team *understands and is committed to what is expected* of a highly effective salesperson. Highly effective sales managers set the direction for success by clearly communicating their expectations. They tell their salespeople what has to happen and why. They communicate not only verbally but also through their actions what is expected to make all their salespeople successful and to help them grow. *Telling* someone does not ensure that they understand or are committed to the expectations. Communicating is more than telling. Communication has to do not only with what we say, but how we say it, and how we respond to the reactions of the person to whom we're saying it. Sales managers who use the five best practices consistently and systematically communicate clearly. Telling, which many people confuse with communication, is basically one-way communication that requires that only the person doing the telling has the ability to speak. There is no obligation on the person being told to do anything but be present. There is no obligation for the person being told to even listen. In fact, telling is a very ineffective way to communicate expectations and get commitment.

What do you expect from your salespeople? Do you take the attitude that your salespeople "know" what you expect? Don't be too sure. When I ask sales managers what they expect from their salespeople, I get various responses. When I then go to the salespeople and ask what their sales managers expect from them, I get their responses, and the two don't usually agree. The expectations of the job are not clearly defined and communicated.

The Job Description

The job description is the starting place for communicating expectations. It wasn't until I worked for Nat that I had a job description. I had worked for three companies and the only thing I knew I was supposed to do was "sell." Nat went over the job description and explained each area. After we discussed each area, I signed it to acknowledge that we had reviewed it. Later I learned the importance of having the salesperson sign the job description. This ensured that I had read it and understood what was expected of me. Having signed the job description ensured the company against possible litigation from me; I couldn't say later on that I didn't know I was supposed to do something.

A job description takes the vagueness out of the job; it gives the sales manager an outline to follow when looking for salespeople; it helps prospective salespeople understand what the job entails; it helps the sales manager in the training and evaluation of the salespeople; it can be the document used to prove that someone the sales manager hired has better qualifications for the job than someone not hired.

Three Areas of a Job Description

A job description basically covers three areas: the primary responsibilities, the essential duties of the job, and the qualifications of the job. These three areas can be no more than a one-page document. Often the only job description some companies have for salespeople is the ad they run to hire a new salesperson. If you have a job description, review it carefully to make sure you can clearly communicate your expectations of each area for the salespersons' jobs (see suggestions below). Then sit down with each salesperson and make sure they understand and commit to what is in it by signing it. Remember that a job description is viewed as a legal document, so anything in it that is seen as discriminatory (race, gender, nationality, age, mental, or physical disabilities) is illegal. If you don't have a job description, write one. There are great resources on the Internet. Go to www.ask.com, www.google.com, or www.yahoo.com and enter "How to write a job description." You'll get several pages of resources to help you prepare one. The following is an example of a job description:

Job Description Example

Primary Responsibility:

Achieves and/or exceeds quota by selling all company products and services to existing and prospective customers in the assigned territory using the company's preferred selling process while adhering to company policies, procedures, and practices.

Essential Duties:

•	Sell and service all company products and services to existing and prospective customers using the company's preferred selling process.

•	Identify prospects in the assigned territory and prepare and execute effective and efficient call plans. Provide weekly call plans and call reports to Sales Manager before start of business Monday mornings.

•	Travel overnight when appropriate, staying within company guidelines for travel costs. Maximize customer/prospect contact time while minimizing travel time and costs.

•	Develop and maintain up-to-date profiles on customers and prospects in the assigned territory.

•	Stay abreast of competition in the territory, and keep Sales Manager and Marketing Manager aware of competitive issues.

- Actively participate in sales, product knowledge, and service meetings.

- Provide quality, personalized service to ensure customer satisfaction and retention.

- Assist administrative personnel with routine and account maintenance, documentation, correspondence, and paperwork required to complete sales. Assist in the preparation of responses to RFPs, written proposals, and presentations.

- Assist in the collection of past due accounts.

- Present a professional image to all customers and prospects in the assigned territory at all times.

- Maintain a positive relationship with all departments of the company.

- Maintain a high level of professionalism by actively participating in and utilizing training.

- Perform all other reasonable related duties as assigned.

Qualifications:

Evidence of emotional intelligence such as initiative, optimism, adaptability, persuasiveness, and achievement drive as shown by results of the company's competency testing process.

Date:_____ Signed by: _____

Communicate Expectations of the Job Description

As you look over the example job description above, I'm sure you can see that there would be a lot of questions that have to be answered in order to explain just the primary responsibility section. For example: how is quota determined? Do I have to be on quota each month, each quarter, or just annually? What if I'm not on quota? What percentage of company products have to be a part of my quota? What is the assigned territory? Is there anyone else selling in that territory from the company? What is the company's preferred selling process? Why does the company have a preferred selling process? Why won't the selling process that I have used for years do since I've been successful with it? Those are just some of the questions from the first paragraph of the example job description. And I'll bet that even if you have a job description now, there are many questions that your salespeople have that need to be reviewed and expectations that need to be clearly communicated.

Prepare, Communicate, Follow-up

Highly effective sales managers communicate expectations by first preparing, then communicating, and then following up.

1.   Prepare to communicate expectations.

      A.   Review your job description thoroughly and make sure that you can explain what each area means. What are your expectations and why? (Just because you're the sales manager isn't a good enough reason. We'll talk more about "why" in a few pages.) Have each salesperson put together their thoughts on what each area means. Meet with upper management to get their input.

B.   Make sure you have clear expectations for each area of the job description. Using the job description example above, clearly define expectations for:

- Achieves or exceeds quota. Is that monthly, quarterly, semi-annually, or just annually? What happens when the salesperson doesn't achieve or exceed quota?

- All company products. What products are included in "all"? What percentage of each product must be sold in order to qualify? In other words, can the salesperson achieve or exceed her quota by selling 100% of product "A" while not selling any of the other products?

- Existing and potential customers. Can the salesperson sell only to existing customers, or must some percentage of potential customers be included? What percentage? Why?

- What is the assigned territory? Is it a geographical area or zip code area? How was it determined? Is there anyone else selling our products in that territory? Why? How does the salesperson interact with those people?

- Company's preferred selling process. What is it? Why does the salesperson have to use it? What if the salesperson doesn't use it?

• Company policies, procedures, and practices. What are these? Where do I find them?

• Prospecting. Do you require accurate, up-to-date records? How accurate and how up-to-date? What are the requirements for regularly adding new business prospects? What prospecting resources (such as directories, newspapers, trade publications, chamber of commerce, and/or associations) are expected to be used? Are there expectations for an appropriate mix of prospects by industry? What are the expectations for telephone prospecting? What are the expectations for scheduling prospecting time?

• Time management. What are the expectations for selling time versus non-selling time activities; territory coverage; appointment scheduling; cold call fill-in; travel?

• Appointments. Are there expectations for the number of appointments weekly; quality of appointments; timing of appointments; appointments with decision makers versus appointments with influencers or users; number of appointments per week, month, year?

• Miscellaneous. Grooming, relationship with home office employees, relationship with management, accurate and timely reporting, service functions, follow-up, maintenance, expanding relationships with current customers.

• Sales. Dollars and/or units generated per product, service, and industry in a given period; accounts opened; expenses; and any other measurable aspect of the job.

C.   After thoroughly investigating and analyzing the job description, determine the expectations that will enable your team to meet your goals.

- Set your expectations high enough to be a challenge, but not so high that it is discouraging and unreachable.

- Document the expectations.

Communicate

2.   In individual and group meetings, communicate your expectations using the job description. Review the input you've gotten from each salesperson and from upper management, consolidate it, and then sit down with your salespeople in groups and individually and review the expectations for each specific area. Work interactively with the salespeople to get commitment to these expectations (that means don't *tell* them but rather review it with them, deal with their ideas and reactions in an affirming, supportive way). Then, have each salesperson sign their job description.

- Communicate with confidence and determination. You've done a lot of work and so has your team. The job description should be something that everyone has had input on.

- Review what your team has agreed on.

- Lay out, in the clearest, most straightforward way possible, exactly what is expected. Don't make people guess. Answer questions, listen, and relate.

• Be open and honest, empowering your people to reach new heights; be encouraging and supportive of teamwork.

• Do what needs to be done without fear of your people not liking you. (Although don't try to deliberately make people dislike you.)

• Let everyone know they are expected to perform according to the job description to accomplish their goals and have fun in the process.

• Communicate expectations about revenue, hours, dress, reports, and sales time versus administrative time, etc.

Follow Up

3.   Follow up. Communicating expectations does not stop in a meeting or one-on-one. It is an ongoing process that requires follow up. Highly effective sales managers follow up by:

• Inspecting what they expect; observing, assessing, and holding people accountable. Having a clear definition of the job description that has been clearly communicated is only the first step; ensuring that everyone is conforming to the job description is the other half. If highly effective sales managers require reports, they make sure they get them complete and on time. They have consequences for non-performers and enforce them with: remedial training, coaching, counseling, probation, termination, and/or redeployment to another area of the company.

• Keeping informed; assessing, observing, listening, working with the individuals and teams. Highly effective sales managers are accessible.

• Not making or accepting blame.

• Doing everything they can to keep their best people and people with promise. They inform those who can't make it that they feel they have gone as far as they are going to go and that they'll work with them to find alternatives for them.

• Proving that they use the process themselves; constantly reinforcing and supporting it by doing what they communicate.

Communicating Expectations Shows the Path

As you can see, communicating expectations lets the sales team know where they stand, where they're going, and how to get there. It is the path to the rest of the best practices. It involves the sales team, letting them share their expectations, getting their feedback, and including them in the process. Without this interactive approach to defining and communicating expectations, the sales team can be highly resistant, demoralized, and disgruntled. Showing them the vision and getting their buy-in is critical to the success of implementing the five best practices. Communicating expectations makes clear to both the sales manager and the salesperson what her job is, what she is supposed to be doing, how she is expected to do it, why it is important to be done, and what needs to be done in order to meet the expectations. It eliminates confusion, one of the most important things a highly effective sales manager does.

A Big Challenge for Sales Managers

One of the biggest challenges sales managers face in implementing the five best practices is in accepting the need to clearly communicate expectations. To lay out what is expected from others almost seems to run against the grain of the way society operates today; "My way is as good as your way." Communicating expectations introduces discipline into the process, and many people are uncomfortable with discipline. Think back to Bert and Phil in the chapter on attitude; neither was comfortable with discipline.

Communicating Expectations and Discipline

Discipline, delivered in a resolute, compassionate manner, is a process where one person is turned into a loyal disciple who follows a leader's guidance. Highly effective sales mangers use resolute and compassionate discipline. Notice the two words used in the preceding sentence: "resolute" and "compassionate." Herb, you'll remember, was certainly resolute, but definitely not compassionate. Phil was compassionate but not resolute. Bert was resolute in following company policy but not compassionate in dealing with his sales team. Highly effective sales managers have a good mixture of both resoluteness and compassion. Nat was an example of such a sales manager: determined, firmly set in his purposes, but also compassionate. This is almost a definition of a highly effective sales manager. According to Webster's College Dictionary, discipline means to "train; a regimen that develops or improves skills." And developing and improving skills and training is what sales managers do. That requires discipline, and discipline starts with clearly communicated expectations.

Discipline Means to Disciple

Many people today cringe at the word "discipline." They think of discipline as punishment with negative connotations. But that is not what I mean by discipline. To discipline someone, one must disciple them. To disciple someone is to make them a pupil or adherent; to lead them through exercises, activities, and a certain regimen that trains or develops skills. Discipline focuses on the positive, on what needs to be done; not on the negative, what is not to be done. If you think back to Chapter 1, Herb was an example of someone who used discipline negatively; he was constantly focused on the negative. Nat was positive; he used discipline by focusing on the positive, on what needed to be done. He discipled me; he made me his pupil.

Discipline Requires Leadership

To bring discipline to an organization or person requires leadership. Highly effective sales managers are leaders. They have no problem making unpopular decisions. They are unequivocal; what they say, they mean. They attack the problems or behaviors, not the people.

They don't try to make people dislike them, but they do not fear making unpopular decisions where some of the sales staff may not like them. Sales managers afraid to make unpopular decisions lack needed leadership skills and have a hard time maintaining discipline and communicating expectations. Sales managers who communicate expectations are leaders who compel their salespeople and teams; they bring discipline to the organization and the individual that develops and improves skills; they are unequivocal; what they say, they mean; they clearly communicate their expectations.

The Effects of Communicating Expectations

Remember the sales managers I talked about in Chapter 1 on Attitude? Two of those sales managers clearly communicated their expectations, but there was a noticeable difference in the effect on each of their sales teams. Herb told us about selling activities that he considered critical, and he expected us to use them. When we tried his method and it didn't work, he berated us. He looked on mistakes as opportunities to criticize, not to coach. Often, Herb would take over when he got frustrated with our attempt to perform the critical sales activities and just do them himself. There was a lot of negative confrontation between Herb and the team. Salespeople didn't see why they "had to do these things." It was clear what Herb wanted but the impact to the team was destructive: low morale, high turnover, and sabotage were the results. Why? Because Herb dictated and demanded but didn't teach; he had rules and consequences. He was always policing.

Nat Communicated Expectations Positively

Nat explained that there were certain selling activities that were critical to optimum sales results. He explained why they were critical and what it would mean not only to the company but also to each person on the sales team individually to use them; how they would help us realize our individual goals. He demonstrated how to use them and worked with the team until we were able to use them skillfully. The impact of Nat's style resulted in high performance, high productivity, high morale, low turnover, and developing salespeople.

Bert Communicated Policies and Prodedures

Bert communicated his expectations about following company procedures and policies; he communicated how important he felt product knowledge was because he talked about it so often. He also communicated his expectations that we do what management wanted done, since that was so very important to him. If he knew there were critical selling activities, he never mentioned them.

Phil Communicated, "Love Me"

Phil communicated his expectation by his manner that everyone get along and "love" him. He was the politician; whatever anyone did was fine; in fact, if you listened to the accolades being given, everyone was doing "great." Like Bert, if Phil knew there were critical selling activities, he never mentioned them.

Sales Managers Are Agents of Change

Highly effective sales managers whole-heartedly subscribe to what Robert J. Calvin said in the quotation I used in the introduction: "The best sales managers realize they are agents of change and, as such they must manage change and change people's behavior." As a highly effective sales manager, we communicate in order to ensure focus and cause change. That means we must clearly communicate our expectations in such a way that everyone understands what they are, why they're important (not only to the company but to each salesperson), how to do them, and are proficient in and committed to doing them.

Communicating Is About Focus

As can be seen, communicating expectations is not gathering the sales team together and painting a picture of what you want. It is about focusing on critical selling activities. Then it is about growing and developing each individual to meet the expectations of those critical selling activities. That means more than telling someone to set five appointments a week. Telling is not the same as making it happen. Telling brings little change, as I have mentioned before. It is a very ineffective communication method because it provides almost no practical learning about how to accomplish what you're telling. Learning how to set appointments requires spending time developing the knowledge and skills in execution, practicing and being supported with positive guidance and reinforcement.

An Example of Telling Ineffectiveness

A good example of the ineffectiveness of telling is shown by one of the exercises I use in my program for sales managers. This exercise helps sales managers begin to understand something about communicating expectations. I open the session by saying:

"We're going to start this session with a little exercise. I'd like everyone to stand up, and hold your arms out parallel to the floor." I demonstrate by stretching my arms out to my sides parallel to the floor, as if I were an airplane getting ready for take off.

"Now, touch the thumb and forefinger of your right hand together to make a circle while keeping your arms outstretched and parallel to the floor." Again, I demonstrate by keeping my arms parallel to the floor and making a circle with my right thumb and forefinger.

"Next, I want you to move your right arm to your face and place the circle you made with your right thumb and forefinger on your chin." As I am saying this, I move my right arm to my face and place the circle made with my thumb and forefinger on my right *cheek*.

Let me ask you a question: Where do you think most of the people in the room place the circle of their thumb and forefinger? On their chin or on their right cheek? If you answered, on their right cheek, you're right. The participants laugh and giggle in embarrassment when they realize they didn't do what they were told.

I've conducted these seminars many times, and always, the vast majority of the people in the room place the circle on their *cheeks*, where I placed mine, and not on their *chins*, as I told them.

What Is Learned from the Exercise

What do you think is learned from this exercise? After the exercise, I ask the participants that question and the predominant answer I get is: "It shows we don't listen too well." That is true, but it's not the major point I want to get across. Lesson number one from this exercise is: What we do and how we do it when communicating is significant. Studies show that we communicate far more with our bodies than with words. 55 percent of the message we send comes from our body language, 38 percent of the message comes from the tone of our voice, and only 7 percent comes from the actual words we use. If our actions are not in congruence with our communication, then we are going to be sending some very mixed messages that will have an often confusing, and just as often, negative impact on our sales teams.

Another Reason for the Exercise

Another reason I conduct this exercise is to emphasize that telling is an inefficient and ineffective way to develop people, and sales management is about developing people. Telling is inefficient because what is told has to be continually repeated, since it's through repetition that others learn. I'm sure you have heard either your father or mother or someone else say, "How many times have I told you..." You fill in the blanks. It's ineffective because people don't listen and don't pay attention, for many reasons. They think they heard what you told them, but didn't catch all the nuances. They're thinking of something else at the time and miss what was said. They don't think you really meant for them to do it, that it's not really important, or that you're just expressing an opinion. Lesson number two from this exercise is this: telling, even repeatedly, is not very effective.

Growing and Developing Individuals and Teams

Communicating expectations happens not only in individual and group meetings, but also in the process of growing and developing individuals and the team to meet these expectations.

Highly effective sales managers maximize the productivity of their sales teams by communicating their expectations that everyone on the team:

- has specific goals

- has a clear understanding of the performance expected of them

- understands why their individual performance is critical to the overall goals for the division or company

- understands how to accomplish what is expected of them

- is capable of accomplishing what is expected of them

- is committed to accomplishing what is expected of them

- has a developmental plan to improve their growth and development as a professional salesperson.

Good Performance Starts with Goals

How important are goals in motivating good performance? Ken Blanchard, author of the *One Minute Manager*, says: "All the research shows that the most important factor in determining good performance starts with goal setting. All good performance starts with clear goals."

There's some interesting validation to Blanchard's statement. A research group was given the project of investigating the impact of goals. In 1979, the graduates of the MBA program at Harvard University were asked by this group: "Have you set clear, written goals for your future and made plans to accomplish them?" The researchers found that three percent of the graduates had written goals and plans; 13 percent had goals, but not in writing; and 84 percent had no specific goals, aside from immediately getting out of school. In 1989, ten years later, the researchers interviewed the members of the class again. They found that the 13 percent who had goals that were not in writing were earning, on average, twice as much as the 84 percent who had no goals. But the three percent who had clear, written goals when they left Harvard were earning, on average, 10 times as much as the other 97 percent ALL TOGETHER. The only difference between the groups was the clarity of the goals they had for themselves when they graduated. Goals do influence performance!

Setting Motivating Goals

I recently had an experience with one of my clients that not only shows the importance of setting goals but also shows the key points in setting goals that motivate. One of my client's salesmen, I'll call him Bill, decided to run a marathon. Once Bill had made that decision, he **made a commitment** to the decision by paying a registration fee, and **let** his wife and **others** on his sales team **know of his decision.** Since a marathon race is 26.2 miles, Bill put together **a plan to train.** He **set daily goals** and **recorded his progress.** This recording allowed him to **evaluate his success toward his ultimate goal.** Throughout his daily training Bill faced several obstacles: a new baby was born, he had an injured knee, and there was a lot of inclement weather at that time of year; but he **maintained his discipline** throughout this period by **relying on others to keep him accountable.** Bill also got an experienced marathon runner to **coach** him. He looked for his coach, as well as his sales team, to keep him accountable. Bill's ultimate goal was to run the marathon in four hours, which he achieved.

As you can see, I highlighted several of the key words in the above paragraph, because they show what must happen for goals to be the motivating force they are meant to be. There must be:

1.   Commitment. A goal is not a goal just because we assign it to someone. The goal must be agreed upon by the person who has the goal to get commitment to the goal. One way we know there is commitment is because the salesperson lets others know about it, just as Bill let his wife and others know. He announced that he was going to achieve this goal.

2.   A plan for how to attain the goal. I can't tell you how often I have said, "I need to lose weight." Yet, I didn't lose any weight because I didn't have a plan. Without a plan, a goal is just a dream. Dreams are nice, but they don't often come to fruition unless there is commitment and a plan to accomplish the dream. Bill had daily activity goals that would lead him to his ultimate goal of running a marathon in four hours. On Mondays and Fridays he rested. On Tuesdays and Thursdays he ran 10 to 13 miles. On Sundays he ran 22 miles. On Wednesdays and Saturdays he ran five to six miles. He put together a special diet. He visualized his goal.

3.   On-going evaluation. Bill set up a method to record his progress daily. This allowed him to know how he was doing and make adjustments when needed.

4.   Discipline. Having a goal and a plan and a record book won't make the goal happen. The person with the goal must have the discipline to do the activities. Given the obstacles that Bill faced (a new baby, an injured knee, and bad weather), it would have been easy for him to back off from his daily training. To do so would have caused him to

miss his ultimate goal. Someone asked Bill at one of the sales meetings how he handled running up hills. Bill replied, "I don't look for hills, but when I come to one, I run it." That's discipline in the face of obstacles. Discipline is required to achieve goals.

5.   Accountability. Bill, his coach, and others on the sales team reviewed the record book with its daily entries. This kept Bill accountable and, as mentioned above, disciplined. Unless there is accountability, it is very easy to slip and miss goals.

6.   Coach. Even the best marathon runners have coaches, because we are not able to see ourselves objectively. Coaches help us see the minor things that when changed, can allow us to reach new heights.

Goals Must Have Commitment

These six points show how to effectively set and meet goals. Because most salespeople do not have clear written goals with plans to achieve those goals, sales managers often have to work with their salespeople to help them develop their goals. Some sales managers set the goals for their salespeople without any input from the sales team. I personally believe that is a mistake. I know we often get our goals "from above" and have to meet them. But we can develop goals to make the goals we received, along with plans to achieve each of our intermediate goals. Goal setting and achievement is much more likely when we take the time to sit down with the salesperson and, using the points outlined above, help them set effective goals with plans to achieve each goal. This process is much more likely to result in commitment by the salesperson to the goal. Without commitment by the salesperson, the possibility of achieving the goal is going to be diminished.

The Importance of Activity Goals

Of course, most salespeople are used to quotas. But many times the only quotas a salesperson has are dollar amount or unit sales quotas. Notice in the six points above for setting and attaining goals, there is one major goal --- run a marathon in four hours --- but there are activity plans that enable the goal to be met. The company may assign a specific quota for a salesperson, but that person can then put together a series of goals and activity plans to ensure achieving that goal. A goal without a plan is a dream, something that I want to accomplish but don't have a focused way to accomplish it. My goal might be to lose 40 pounds. The activity plan that enables me to lose 40 pounds includes:

- Determining how many calories or carbohydrates I will consume each day and stick with that number of calories or carbohydrates

- Determining how much exercise I will perform each day and perform that exercise consistently

- Determining how much water I will drink each day and drink that amount

- Setting up an accountability process to ensure that I stick with the calories/carbohydrates, exercise, and water, and use someone who will help me be accountable.

A great many steps make up the ultimate achievement of a goal. To accomplish goals requires developing and managing a process for achieving the goal, and that means managing the activities and behavior of the person who has set the goal.

Benefits of Activity Goals

There are several benefits to converting annual goals into smaller activity tasks:

• Monthly, weekly, and daily goals are more easily understood and managed; they clarify the level of activity needed to meet the goals.

• Smaller goals allow the sales manager and salesperson to spot potential shortfalls long before they occur. The sales manager is better able to provide assistance when the shortfall is realized early in the year compared to late in the year.

• Since results follow behavior, focusing on the right activities daily, weekly, and monthly cause the desired long-term result.

Setting Activity Goals

Backing into activity goals is accomplished by reviewing the number of activities necessary to accomplish a goal. Let's say that on the average, for every 10 appointments a salesperson gets, she closes two sales. How many phone calls does it take to get 10 appointments? Let's say that it takes 100 phone calls to get 10 appointments. How many phone calls does she need to make every day in order to get her 10 appointments per week? Dividing 100 phone calls by five days in a week shows that she will need to make 20 phone calls a day in order to get her 10 appointments per week. 20 phone calls becomes her daily activity goal. She then develops a plan to ensure that she makes these 20 phone calls a day and has someone who will help her be accountable to the process. This is one of those areas where people often say, "sales is a numbers game." The point is, use some strategy in the numbers to improve the overall impact.

Setting Activity Goals May Require Training

Some salespeople struggle with the idea of activity goals. Often, the reason for this struggle is that they lack the skills in the necessary activities to achieve the results wanted. Highly effective sales managers focus on this lack, and make it a priority in the salesperson's development. That might mean that the sales manager does a lot of one-on-one training and coaching the person who lacks the necessary skills. Or, the sales manager might get the salesperson some special training with follow-up by the sales manager.

Goal Setting Is an Opportunity to Communicate

Highly effective sales managers understand that goal setting is an opportunity to communicate their expectations. When the sales manager and the salesperson agree to both ultimate dollar and activity goals, the message is clear about the responsibility and the criteria for goal achievement. Salespeople want to understand not only what their responsibility is, but what criteria will be used to evaluate their progress in the responsible area. When goals include both dollar amounts and activities, they identify not only the responsibility of the salesperson (the dollar amount to achieve) but also the criteria for achieving that responsibility. Both parts are important in clear goals. An example would be when the sales manager and the salesperson agree that the salesperson must generate $30,000 this month and will make 10 prospect calls per week. This identifies that "prospecting" is the responsibility of the salesperson, and "10 prospect calls per week" identifies the criteria for fulfilling the prospecting responsibility. Or, the prospecting criteria might be a percentage of appointments, such as when the salesperson agrees that he will maintain 10 prospects for every one appointment set.

Why Two Parts to the Goal?

Why two parts to the goal? Identifying the responsibility and the criteria ensures that both the salesperson and the sales manager are in agreement; no one gets a surprise when the salesperson's assessment happens. Assessing means to determine value and every salesperson wants to know his or her value and how that value will be determined. By including both parts, responsibility and criteria, the questions salespeople have get answered. Salespeople want to know:

1.   What do you expect me to do?

2.   Why should I do it?

3.   How do you want me to do it?

4.   What will indicate that I did it well?

Smart Goals

Goal setting can be a motivating factor for salespeople if the goals are SMART:

> • Specific. Be specific and avoid generalities. "10 appointments per week" is specific; "getting appointments" is not. The more specific a goal is the better. Generalities leave too much room for interpretation of the goal, which may invite resistance, confusion, and disillusionment during any assessment.

> • Measurable. A goal is measurable if the salesperson can apply specific numbers or other observable indicators of performance to the goal. Rates (65 percent of annual goal accomplished by the end of second quarter), ranges (plus or minus 10 percent of expense budget in any one quarter), quantities (10 appointments per week) are all measurable activities (getting the prospect to introduce the salesperson to the decision maker). Qualitative measures are more subjective, such as a customer's or the sales manager's opinion. To include the measurable attribute requires some method of tracking performance or defining results.

> • Attainable. If a salesperson is working with a large prospect company that is going to have several people involved in the buying decision, and the salesperson has set a goal of closing the

business on the first call, is that attainable? Attainable should not be easy, but should have some stretch built in. If the salesperson has always set 10 appointments per week, maybe it's time to go for 11 or 12.

• Realistic. Is it realistic to consider the goal set? Goals for new salespeople are often lower than goals for experienced salespeople. If there are circumstances that are going to influence the reality of making a goal, that should be considered also. An example might be for a senior salesperson the sales manager relies on to do coaching and mentoring. What impact will those coaching and mentoring tasks have on the reality of the senior salesperson making the goal? I have found that at times I have to negotiate activity goals down because of the eagerness of the salesperson. Salespeople are often so optimistic and eager that they will set unrealistic goals.

• Time-defined. Goals should have a specific deadline or date of completion, just as Bill's goal was to "run the Marathon being held on March 2nd in four hours." Deadlines give the sales manager a basis for evaluation of progress and feedback. Long-term goals should have milestones or review dates the sales manager can use as coaching opportunities with the salesperson. 10 appointments "this week" is time-defined; 10 appointments is not. Put a time on it. I'm sure that Bill, my client's salesperson, could run 26 miles if he had several days to do it. But he chose to limit himself to four hours in a Marathon on a specific date.

Annual Goals Are Less Effective

Sales teams that set only annual goals have the lowest rate of meeting or exceeding their sales goals. Sales teams that set goals more frequently—whether monthly, quarterly or semi-annually—have a significantly greater success rate in meeting their sales goals. Goal setting on a more frequent basis often helps salespeople to remain focused on meeting their objectives.

Communicating Critical Sales Performance Expectations

There are certain sales performance activities and behaviors that are critical to producing sales success that need to be communicated. They include but are not necessarily limited to: Finding prospects, making appointments, pre-call planning, developing rapport with prospects and customers, qualifying prospects, asking effective questions that determine needs, presenting solutions that show value to the prospect, handling objections, closing, and post-call follow-up. You might have others in your industry, but the point is that unless these critical activities are performed efficiently and effectively, sales success will not be optimized. Highly effective sales managers have performance expectations because they provide a standard by which to judge everyone equally. Highly effective sales managers:

1. *know* what performance is critical to produce sales success

2. communicate *what* performance is critical and *why* it is critical

3. *demonstrate* what performance is critical in such a way that the salesperson can do it

4. provide the salesperson with the *value of that performance that is important to him or her* so that the salesperson will perform the critical activity

Step One: Know What Performance Is Critical

First, the Sales manager must *know* what performance is critical to produce sales success. Knowing the selling process is the first step to being able to communicate your expectations of it and to teach it. By "knowing" I mean being able to break it down into learnable steps that can be explained, demonstrated, and the value of each step for the salesperson discussed.

Many sales managers were the selling stars of their company. They're like Joan, a sales manager I worked with. Everyone called her a "natural born salesperson." Joan was very good at *doing* the critical selling activities. But as a sales manager, *doing* is not what is important now; *developing* people is what is important.

The point here is, "Does Joan *know* what the critical selling activities are?" When asked, she couldn't explain what she did that made her successful as a salesperson. When working with salespeople who needed to know what to do, Joan would say, "Just watch what I do and do that." Since there's only one Joan and nobody else can be Joan, that tactic failed. Both Joan and her sales team were frustrated, and she was having turnover issues. That creates a double problem. If the problem isn't fixed, the company could lose not only some excellent potential salespeople, but Joan as well. Joan might return to the world of selling, but with another company, and others leave because they aren't improving, which was my problem with Bert and Phil. Joan's first task was to define the critical selling activities so that *she could communicate her expectations about them and explain them to others.* This sets her up to define her intuitive talents and multiply herself. It's like cloning your best person. The beauty of this process is it not only enables the non-superstars to improve, but it makes the superstars even more successful when they use it. The point is highly effective sales managers must know the critical selling activities.

Doing Versus Developing

Because Joan couldn't verbalize what she expected, she couldn't communicate performance expectations. She found herself often taking over a sale when she was with one of her salespeople. She had fallen into the trap that many sales managers fall into: *doing* instead of *developing*. One of the major complaints against sales managers by salespeople is that they "take over the sale" when making joint calls.

There are times when it would have been appropriate for Joan, or any sales manager, to be doing the selling, if the goal of the call is for that salesperson to see "how it's done." But unless the goal of the call is for the salesperson to observe some particular aspect of the selling process that will be discussed after the call, the sales manager should let the salesperson do the selling.

Why Sales Managers Take Over the Sale

Why do Joan and so many other sales managers take over calls when they're with their salespeople? I'm convinced that there are two major reasons: first, the sales manager has not made the shift from salesperson mentality to a coaching mentality necessary for an effective sales manager; second, the sales manager has not learned how to define the selling process to adequately teach it to the salesperson. Even though many sales managers were very good salespeople and intuitively understand what needs to be done in the selling process, they have never learned how to break each of the steps down into a teachable process.

Document the Best Practices

Highly effective sales managers identify and document selling skills. Becoming expertly versed in these skills allows the sales manager to be able to see exactly what's going on with their salespeople, to assess what they are doing well, and determine what needs improvement. The better the sales manager understands the selling process, the more accurate the observations. The more accurate the observations, the more effective the sales manager can be at improving his or her salespeople's deficiencies, which can result in higher, more profitable sales.

- Document the most effective way for:

  ➢ Building rapport. Understanding and dealing with different behavior types, rapport-building techniques, putting prospects at ease, building trust and credibility, and setting expectations.

> ➢ Exploring needs. Transitioning to asking questions; using questions appropriately to determine needs; identifying decision makers and influencers; qualifying for time, money, and need; identifying needs; summarizing, prioritizing, and confirming needs.

> ➢ Presentations. Number of presentations per week, month, year; quality of presentations; presentations' appropriateness to needs; interesting presentations; interactive presentations; visuals; individual versus group presentations.

> ➢ Handling concerns. Recognizing concerns, empathizing, non-argumentative methods, understanding concerns, confirming resolution of concerns, meeting objections.

> ➢ Closing. Asking for the business, asking for next steps.

Once the most effective selling skills are documented, share those with the whole team and work to ensure that everyone is using them.

Step Two: Communicate

Second, the sales manager must communicate to his salespeople what performance is critical and why it is critical. Let me give you an example for this second point that I have used in the past. One of the critical selling activities is prospecting, so I explain to my team the need for everyone to prospect on a regular basis (my expectation). But I don't stop with just explaining the need to prospect. I go through an exercise to show why prospecting is important. That exercise would sound something like this:

"Using our average sales of $X, how many sales do we need to make in order to make our numbers this month?" I ask.

After I get the number, I ask, "How many presentations does it take for us to make one sale?"

Again, after I get the number, I ask, "How many appointments do we have to make in order to get to make a presentation?"

"And," I continue after getting that number, "how many calls to prospects do we have to make in order to get that number of appointments?"

"What happens to our ultimate number if we don't make the number of prospect calls that got us the appointments that allowed us to make a presentation that got us the dollars we need to make our numbers?" By now it's pretty clear why prospecting is important and that I expect it to be done on a regular basis.

The method I just showed introduces my expectations about prospecting, but my communicating is not finished with just introducing. I further communicate my expectation for prospecting by following the remaining four other best practices of sitting with salespeople to observe their prospecting, assessing their prospecting effectiveness, coaching them when their prospecting was not as effective as needed, and in general, through all of this, holding them accountable for prospecting by inspecting what I expect.

It's Not "Know and Tell"

Just knowing the critical activities and just telling your salespeople these are critical activities is not enough. The sales manager must communicate in a way that helps the salesperson understand and buy into why these activities are critical. Remember, success in selling comes from doing the critical activities consistently and well. Selling inconsistently but well won't make for optimum success. Selling consistently and poorly won't make for optimum success either. Salespeople who know what the activities are and why they are important are much more likely to perform them consistently and well.

Step Three: Demonstrate

Third, sales managers must be able to demonstrate to each salesperson how to accomplish what performance is critical in such a way that the *salesperson* can accomplish it. To improve salespeople who are not performing to their abilities requires that sales managers develop this critical third sales manager fundamental. "But," you say, "I've been making presentations and doing demonstrations for ages. I know how to demonstrate." That's all well and good, but the point here is to *demonstrate so that the salesperson can do it, not just so that the salesperson knows how you do it.* As a sales manager, you're really putting on your training hat now.

Communicating Through Training

One of the most important things highly effective sales managers do is training. An effective training method highly effective sales manager use is the five-step method shown below:

1.   Explain what you want them to do and why it's important, both to them and to the organization.

2.   Show them how to do it.

3.   Allow them to try to do it.

4.   Observe them as they try.

5.   Praise success or any movement toward success. If they don't get it right, go back through steps two through five.

Don't Skip Steps Three Through Five

As salespeople doing presentations and demonstrations, we often do steps one and two above. However, we're now training salespeople to be able to do something they weren't able to do before. That takes steps three through five. It also takes a lot of patience on the sales manager's part, because we're comfortable showing and telling and assuming they have it. Usually salespeople don't have it with just showing and telling. They need to practice where the sales manager can observe, provide positive feedback on what part they do well, and re-instruct them on the part they didn't do so well. Then, the salesperson needs to take the skill back to the field and show they can apply it. It is only through this continuing process that we train people in skills. Understanding something intellectually does not mean we are able to apply what we understand. Understanding how a guitar is manufactured is not the same as being able to manufacture one, nor is the ability to play a guitar the same as the ability to communicate to someone else how to play one. The point here again is to be able to demonstrate the critical activity in such a way that the salesperson can do it, not just that we can demonstrate or explain it.

Step Four: Show the Value

Fourth, the sales manager must show or tie the value that is important to the salesperson to what is critical so that he or she *will* perform it. Just as prospects want to know "What's in it for me?" when we explain our products or services, salespeople want to know the same thing when we communicate our expectations that they start doing an activity they have either not been performing or improve an activity they have not been performing well. Just as customers are looking for what's in it for them, so too are salespeople.

Many sales managers show their salespeople what needs to be done, why it should be done, and how it should be done, but don't tie it to the value to the individual salesperson. It's like a salesperson that shows what the product is, why he is showing it to the prospect, and how it is used, but doesn't tie all of that to the value to the prospect and then ask for the business. Those salespeople lose many sales. This fourth point can be likened to focusing on the value to this particular prospect and asking for the business or closing. It is at this step that we determine whether the salesperson sees "What's in it for him" and is "buying." Sales managers stand a better chance of the salesperson committing to the expectations when she is shown how it will fill a value important to her and is asked for a commitment.

Check for Commitment

Trial closes work very effectively here to show the sales manager how close he is to making the sale with the individuals on the sales team to the expectations communicated. Some typical questions that the sales manager can use at this step are:

1.   How does that sound to you?

2.   How do you feel about that?

3.   What effect do you see this having on your goal of _____?

Any tentative answer by the salesperson is an opportunity for the sales manager to probe more deeply to understand the concern or lack of understanding of what's in it for the salesperson. It is at this step that if the salesperson has a concern it will typically be voiced. Or, if it isn't voiced, there will be some indication he isn't buying into the request. Until the salesperson sees the value in what you're asking him to do, there will not be buy-in and use of the activity. When salespeople "buy in" they are not only vested in the idea, they are committed to the process: be it yours or their own. Most salespeople are pretty comfortable with what they're already doing. Even though they have been shown what to do, why it needs to be done, how it should be done, and have demonstrated they can do it doesn't mean they will. You're asking them to change and changing behavior is uncomfortable. Yet we know the price of success is discomfort! Changing behaviors is a challenge. Salespeople get comfortable doing things a certain way, and now they are being asked to change. People resist change. Resistance is the sales manager's biggest challenge.

Confirming Commitment Is Critical

Many sales managers are reluctant to put this critical fourth point to work and confirm the commitment by the salesperson. Just as many salespeople do not ask for the business for fear of getting a "no," sales managers do not ask. It's much easier just to assume that because we explained what to do, why it is important, and showed them how to do it that the salesperson will now do what we've asked. Not practicing this fourth point is like going through the entire selling process with a prospect and not stressing value and not asking for the business. Some prospects will intuitively see the value and close the business for you, but too many don't, and we lose valuable sales by not asking.

Use Your Sales Skills to Determine Your Team's Values

As I said previously, most sales managers were very good salespeople, which means that they know how to ask questions and gather information. Gathering information about what your salespeople value is important to using this fourth step successfully. This information becomes a tool to help salespeople become more effective.

Sales managers who can answer the following questions in the affirmative are ready to be responsible and accountable for growing and developing their salespeople:

1.   Do I know what critical selling activities result in optimum sales?

2.   Am I able to communicate these critical activities to my salespeople and focus on why they are important?

3.   Do I understand how to accomplish each of the critical activities, and am I able to demonstrate how to others in a way that they can perform it?

4.   Do I know the values of my salespeople, and am I able to relate these critical activities to them from their value perspective in a way that will motivate them to perform?

The Sales Manager's Main Goal

The sales manager's main goal is to build salespeople who achieve the levels of sales volume, profits, and growth desired by higher levels of management. The factor underlying a sales manager's success in achieving this goal is the ability to influence the behavior of all parties involved. This includes the sales manager's ability to influence salespeople to do things they would not do on their own. Defining and clearly communicating expectations is the first best practice used by highly effective sales managers to achieve this main goal. By now, it should be clear that communicating expectations takes time, collaboration, and patience. It isn't something that is done quickly or once. Good communication happens through planning and repetition. In the next chapter we'll look at observing, the second best practice of highly effective sales managers. Observing helps sales managers understand if they clearly communicated their expectations.

chapter three

Best Practice #2: Observe On-The-Job Performance

Several years ago, Tom Peters wrote a book titled *In Search of Excellence*[1]. In that book he coined a phrase: "Managing by walking around." What he meant by this phrase was that managers of excellent organizations take the time to get out of their offices and walk around the workplace so that they can observe what is happening first hand. They get out where the workers are and observe what is going on. They get involved at the point of customer contact or at the point where the employee is applying his skills to the job.

At about the same time that Peters wrote his book, Ken Blanchard wrote the book *One Minute Manager*[2]. In Blanchard's book, he coined a

---

1 Thomas J. Peters, Robert H. Waterman, Jr., *In Search of Excellence* (Warner Books, Inc., 1982)

phrase: "Catch people doing something right." What Blanchard meant by his phrase enlarged on Peter's concept: be among your people on a regular basis so that you can observe what your people are doing, and when you see them doing something right, or even *attempting* to do something right, praise them. That praise is what clearly communicates your expectations and reinforces those expectations. When they aren't doing something right, since you've observed them, you have an opportunity to re-direct them, another opportunity to clearly communicate expectations. We'll talk more about re-directing in the chapter on coaching.

Coaches Make Use of Observation

Coaches in the worlds of sports and entertainment, like highly effective sales managers, are professional developers of people who make extensive use of observation. They do very little lecturing, inspiring, or even shouting at their players (contrary to what you sometimes see on TV!). What they do is a lot of watching during performance and after performance via videotape. They observe their players' movements in great detail. They observe during practice as well as during performances. They look for idiosyncrasies of their player's performance, and keep meticulous records of that performance. They gather data to be utilized for improving performance. When they see a player consistently making an error such as a football player who has his feet out of position or who isn't wrapping his arms around the opponent in order to tackle him,

---

2 .Kenneth Blanchard, Ph.D., Spencer Johnson, M.D., *The One Minute Manager* (Blanchard Family Partnership and Candle Communications Corporation, 1982).

they tell him about it, walk him through the proper procedure, watch him as he does it again, and praise him when he finally masters it.

Just like professional coaches, highly effective sales managers bring out the best in their salespeople through careful observation, information gathering, feedback, patient dialogue, correct instruction and using positive reinforcement when things go well.

What to Do After Observing

The paragraph explaining what professional coaches do above is a blueprint for the power of observation and what needs to be done after one observes. Notice what professional coaches do *not* do: very little lecturing, inspiring, or shouting at their players. That's not the typical stereotype of a coach, is it? Many of us think that all coaches do is lecture, inspire, and shout! We often think of a frustrated coach yelling and shouting at a player who made a mistake when we think of coaches. But that's not what makes highly successful professional coaches successful.

The secret to success is in the watching—observing actions and behaviors in great detail. It is only by observing that professional coaches, and highly effective sales managers, determine if they have clearly communicated their expectations and that they are being carried out. And that's a significant point. Highly effective sales managers first communicate their expectations and then follow up with observing.

What to Watch For

Notice what professional coaches watch for: their players' movements in great detail . . . the idiosyncrasies of their players' performance. Professional coaches know that the way a football player moves indicate his effectiveness as a player. They also know that players will automatically add their own individual idiosyncrasies to what has been communicated. So long as those individual idiosyncrasies didn't detract from the players' performance, the coaches don't focus on them. It is when they are detrimental to performance that professional coaches react. This is also true of highly effective sales managers. They watch their salespeople's "movements and idiosyncrasies," the way they use the selling process, to determine their effectiveness. So long as those movements are not detrimental, there is no reason to react. It is when they cause less than optimum performance that the highly effective sales manager takes corrective action.

Keep Track of Observations

The highly effective sales manager keeps records and charts on each salesperson's performance and uses that data to determine developmental opportunities or opportunities for reward and recognition. We'll talk more about gathering and using data in the chapter on assessing strengths and limitations.

What to Work On

Notice also from the paragraph above who the professional coaches work with to correct: they focus on players consistently making errors. That doesn't imply that coaches never observe players who don't consistently make errors. You can be sure that professional coaches observe all their players—All-Americans as well as second stringers. Top performers like to know that the head man is aware of what they're doing and how they do it. That's why highly effective sales managers don't devote all their time to only poor, marginal, or moderate performers.

Sometimes sales managers think that the only people they have to observe and work with are the ones who are not performing or who are marginal performers. Highly effective sales managers know differently. They understand that even top performers know that they can get even better when someone who has a coach's attitude comes along. They also know that everyone can improve, no matter how good they are, and observing shows the sales manager where improvements can be made.

How to Use Observation for Growth and Development

Notice how professional coaches work to develop players. When they see a player consistently making an error, then they get activated. They tell him about it, walk him through the proper procedure, watch him do it again, and congratulate him for mastery when he does it the right way. There are some keys in this statement that show sales managers how to be effective at helping someone improve performance:

1.   We have to *see* the player making *consistent* errors. If we don't observe (see) it, then it's very difficult to know what is happening and how to correct it.

2.   The problem needs to be consistent. Traveling with a salesperson one time and observing her, and thinking that everything she does during that time is the way she always does it isn't realistic. To see what is happening takes several observations to understand the difference between what is consistent and what is a one-time happening.

3.   We have to tell them about it. Someone can't correct something if they don't know about it. Many sales managers are afraid to tell someone that they have an area that needs correcting. There is always the possibility of confrontation and that is distasteful to the Bert's and Phil's of the world. Confrontation, like attitude, is another word that is often thought of negatively. Yet what confrontation means is to "meet face to face; to bring together for examination or comparison," which is an important part of being a highly effective sales manager. Dr. Henry Cloud and Dr. John Townsend, psychologists, wrote in their book, *How People Grow*[3], "Confrontation is an important tool to get someone to see his inability to change and to see his need for help. Many people are too soft-hearted; they give *encouragement* to someone who needs *discouragement* instead. To encourage a powerless person to try harder is one of the worst things you could possibly do." Phil was an example of someone who gave encouragement when what was needed was discouragement. And confrontation should never be used like Herb used it destructively. It should always be a part of the nurturing of the individual. Walk them through the proper procedure. Here's

---

[3] Dr. Henry Cloud & Dr. John Townsend, *How People Grow* (Zondervan, 2001).

where the sales manager must be able to demonstrate how to do it, and demonstrate it in such a way that the salesperson can do it.

4.   Watch them try the new way. This is a very important key. Once we show the person how to do it in such a way that *they* can do it we give them the chance to show us they can do it. We watch them while they're performing this new way. As I have said numerous times before in this book, telling is ineffective. We have to see that what we told them has been received and they can do it.

5.   Give them a "well done" for mastery or go back through steps two to five of the training process we discussed on page 53 again. Mastery of a correct procedure may take a couple of tries. It is important that we be supportive as the person tries this new way of doing something. Positive reinforcement is critical at this point, even if they don't get it mastered right away. Encourage even attempts at the new procedure. This point is akin to encouraging a baby to go from crawling to walking. As the baby shakily stands and attempts to take one step, we shout encouragement. If the baby gets one step completed and then falls, we are generous in our praise. We don't say, "You didn't walk over to the sofa, you only walked one step!" Keep encouraging until you get their best. Don't settle for less than their best! And if they totally don't get it, go back to step 1 of the training process, explain, demo, let them practice, observe, and give them feedback. That's what a good coach and a highly effective sales manager does.

An Important Point for New Sales Managers

There's an important point to be made here, especially for new sales managers who may have salespeople on their teams who are far and away better salespeople than the sales manager ever was. The point is that many professional coaches whom we have never heard about coach football stars like Peyton Manning, one of the best quarterbacks in the game. They also coach many other outstanding football players even though they personally could never play as well as any of the players. An example that comes to mind is Jon Gruden, currently the NFL head coach of Tampa Bay. Jon Gruden realized early on that he was too small to play college or professional football, but he had a vision to coach. In his first year as the head coach at Tampa Bay he took the Buccaneers to the Super Bowl and won. The point is that anyone with a coach's attitude can observe another person, and using the methodology outlined in the five steps in communicating through training on page 53 and the coaching techniques shown in Chapter5, can help that person.

Observation Opportunities

There are various opportunities to observe salespeople's proficiency in selling. Sales managers can observe their salespeople during:

> • Training sessions, where selling skills are practiced. When sales managers use outside consultants or training organizations or some other group in the company to train, it is critically important that the sales manager attend and reinforce that training once the salespeople come back on the job. We talked in Chapter 2 about the ineffectiveness of training when it is not reinforced on the job.

• Sales meetings, when discussions come up about calls and how the salesperson handled the call. These are great opportunities for the sales manager to have the individuals use the exact verbiage that was used on the call, and do some observing and coaching.

• Role-play sessions either with the sales manager or with another salesperson. The sales manager or other salesperson plays the part of the prospect and has the salesperson "sell" him. At first this can be somewhat uncomfortable for the salesperson, but if continued and handled positively as we'll discuss in the chapter on coaching, it can be an important way to improve skills.

• Joint calls. This is the best place to observe salespeople because it is an example of how that salesperson really performs. Again, as I said above, the sales manager will have to make several joint calls with the salesperson before seeing a pattern that needs to be discussed and corrected.

Critical Guidelines for Making Joint Calls

Speaking of making joint calls, there are some things that highly effective sales managers do that are critical to follow:

1.   Determine before the call the role the sales manager will play. When the purpose of a joint call is for the sales manager to observe the salesperson's selling skills, it is important that the sales manager not take over the sale. In the pre-call planning session, the salesperson and the sales manager clearly establish what role each of them is going to play on this call. The sales manager will need to bring up some situations so that everyone is clear about who does what. One such situation is, "If

the prospect asks me (sales manager) a question, I'll refer him to you (salesperson) for the answer."

2.   Don't violate the salesperson's credibility in front of the prospect. It is important that the salesperson's credibility is not put at risk with his prospects. The sales manager will leave after the call, but the salesperson has to continue calling on this prospect. Taking over the call will only end up with the sales manager responsible for doing what the salesperson already gets paid to do.

3.   Determine how you will explain the presence of the sales manager. The assumption many prospects make when a sales manager is along is that the salesperson is a novice and needs help. That may be true, but highly effective sales managers don't say that. They say something like, "I like to get to know our customers and prospective customers, so I travel with my salespeople periodically. Today I'm with Joan."

What do highly effective sales managers look for when they are observing their salespeople? They look for how effectively the salesperson is using critical selling activities and behaviors that have been communicated. Observing helps sales managers make others successful; it shows the sales manager where to facilitate individual development and coach for opportunities. In order to be aware of salespeople's sales skills, highly effective sales managers observe the salespeople interacting with customers and prospects. They inspect what they expect. The best way to observe a salesperson is on a joint call. However, it takes several observations during several calls to come to any true conclusion about a salesperson's people skills.

Highly Effective Sales Managers Are Observant

Highly effective sales managers are observant; they pay attention to details, just as professional coaches do. Being observant is more, though, than just seeing and hearing what is happening. Highly effective sales managers are aware of what *isn't* said as well as what *is*. They observe not only the words used but also the body language and tone of voice. Remember, as I said previously, body language and tone play a more important point in communication than words. Observing is a way of ensuring that your salespeople know that you are paying attention, that you care, and that you want to help.

In the next chapter, we'll look at assessing strengths and determining developmental areas.

chapter four

Best Practice #3: Assess Strengths & Opportunities for Growth

To assess something is to determine its value. Our people are the most valuable resource we have, and continually assessing that resource is a critical part of what highly effective sales managers do to ensure they have the best resources at all times. Highly effective sales managers determine their salespeople's strengths and areas that need development in order to assess their current value and to determine how to help them raise their value. Notice that the preceding sentence focuses on assessing where the salesperson is right now, and determining how to raise the salesperson to a different level. Assessing is more than just providing salespeople with information about their results. It is about using information to determine how to go about raising the salesperson's value. Assessing allows the sales manager to determine underlying barriers that are keeping the salesperson from being all that she can be. Once the underlying barriers are discovered, the salesperson and the sales manager develop strategies to remove those barriers and increase the salesperson's value.

Assessing Happens Continually

The highly effective sales manager is constantly assessing her salespeople to determine how they are doing and what needs to be done to improve them. She looks at not only the salesperson's individual performance but also the business results that performance generates. It is about planning for the future, setting and achieving expectations, developing salespeople, problem solving, and motivation. Assessing is more than a quarterly, semi-annual, or annual performance appraisal. Waiting until a quarter to determine and act on problems or to start development of needed skills is too long. Assessing happens constantly, day-by-day, week-by-week. Of course quarterly, semi-annual, or annual performance appraisals are a part of the assessing process. However, highly effective sales managers assess and plan remedies constantly.

The Benefits of Assessing

Assessing salesperson value has many benefits:

- It gives the salesperson and the sales manager direction. Discovering an area for development allows the salesperson and the sales manager to work together to move in a new direction that will attain higher results.

• It's an opportunity to set new goals. The salesperson, when appraised of a particular area, can set goals to work on that area. Or, when strengths are assessed and achieved, the salesperson can take on higher goals.

• It enables the salesperson to know that the sales manager cares. Knowing that the sales manager cares is a significant motivating factor for salespeople that can reduce turnover and improve productivity.

• It helps to clarify expectations. During an assessment session, the sales manager and the salesperson discuss activities and behaviors. Often what results from this discussion is the understanding that expectations weren't clear, and that leads to unwanted results. Assessment sessions can clarify expectations.

• It gets buy-in from the salesperson on needed development. Looking at results and the activities and behaviors that caused those results, especially when the results were not at the expected level, provides an opportunity to get buy-in and commitment from the salesperson.

• Helps plan for the future. Assessment sessions are future oriented; they're focused not only on what is going well, but what needs to be done differently in order to grow. When salespeople grow, the company grows and can make better plans.

Include Measurement Indicators

Assessment is about "How am I doing?" There should be no surprises here if there were clear expectations and specific measurement indicators. That means that each performance expectation needs a measurement indicator. What are some measurement indicators?

- Quantity. Dollars of sales, number of calls, number of appointments, number of closed sales, units sold, expense at budget or off budget.

- Quality. Customer satisfaction ratings, internal departmental ratings.

- Project milestones. Moving the sale from an original call to the next step, attending a training program, completing a team assignment, meeting an improvement goal.

- Deadlines. Submitting call plans, call reports, expense reports on time. Accounts receivables within 30 days.

- Increased knowledge. Learning the product features and benefits and being able to use them effectively.

Highly effective sales managers work with their salespeople to develop the indicators, thereby creating another opportunity for relationship building between both. Using the job description, communicated expectations, observations and feedback on the salesperson's activities, behaviors, and attitude on the job allows the sales manager and the salesperson to work together in assessing performance.

Assessing: Measuring Progress

Assessing has to do with measuring progress toward agreed upon objectives and goals. These objectives and goals were determined and agreed upon when the sales manager reviewed the job description, in the on-going process of communicating expectations, and through the growth and development plans agreed upon. The sales manager and the salesperson review and agree on specific objectives in addition to specific goals in:

1.   The objectives of the job description. The job description outlines the salesperson's primary responsibilities, the essential duties, and the qualifications of the job. The job description answers the salesperson's question, "What do you want me to do?" The job description might read, "Meet or exceed sales objectives by selling widgets and other services in the assigned territory." The sales manager continually assesses how well the salesperson is covering the territory selling widgets.

   • Is the salesperson meeting sales objectives but only covering part of the territory? How? Why?

   • Is the salesperson covering all the territory but not meeting sales objectives? Why?

   • Is the salesperson selling widgets and other services or just widgets? Why?

2.   Activities and behaviors compared to expectations that were communicated. The sales manager and salesperson may have agreed to appointment activities as "Make 10 appointments per week with new prospects." This answers the salesperson's question, "How do you want

me to do my job?" The sales manager continually assesses how well the salesperson is meeting the goal of 10 appointments with new prospects per week.

- Are there ten appointments being made per week? What is the quality of the appointments? Are those appointments with new prospects? How many of those appointments are resulting in bona fide opportunities for sales?

3. Growth and development goals. The sales manager and the salesperson may have set a goal to improve the salesperson's skills for handling objections. Through observation of the salesperson during a prospect call and by a review of the salesperson's closed sales, the sales manager will assess how successfully the salesperson is meeting this goal.

- Is the salesperson using the methods discussed in the coaching session? How well is the salesperson using them? Are they working? Why? Why not?

When sales managers work with salespeople on their growth and development, they answer the question of how to do an activity or use a behavior and why.

4. Sales goals. Goals the salesperson has for generating dollars or units of products and services are continually assessed.

- Are these goals above target, on target, below target? Why are they where they are? Do they contain the right mix? Are they sold into the right industry?

5. Weekly plans. As we have seen, goals without plans are not very effective. The sales manager continually assesses the effectiveness of the salesperson's plans for making his goals.

> • Are the plans well thought out? Are they effective? Do they result in the goals being made? If not, why?

This assessment goes on continually by the sales manager.

Assess Attitude

In addition to these areas, the salesperson's attitude toward work, team members, other employees in the company, customers, prospects, and the sales manager is continually assessed. Salespeople, like the sales manager, want to know how they are doing. Assessing helps them to know the answer.

Compare Actuals to Goals

All of these areas are assessed by comparing them to goals. Some of that progress is made through observation during calls, sales meetings, coaching sessions, feedback from customers, prospects, team members, and other employees in the company; and some from reports.

Track Progress Against Goals

When sales managers assess a salesperson's performance, they are assessing the salesperson's ability to accomplish the goals necessary to sustain and grow the salesperson as well as the organization. Highly effective sales managers measure and track their salespeople's progress toward goals on a regular basis. They observe, coach, supervise, and instruct in order to cause selling improvements needed because of assessments they have made. Highly effective sales managers know selling success isn't achieved by selling at the same level consistently. They know selling success is achieved by selling at higher levels than in the past. The key to accomplishing higher selling levels is achieved through on-going development and assessment of that development. Some of the questions they ask to determine growth and development are:

1. Are sales improving?

2. Is the backlog of potential sales improving?

3. Is there evidence of improvement in the areas that are being coached?

4. Does the salesperson have the attitude necessary for success?

5. Is the salesperson motivated to do the job necessary for success?

6. Does the salesperson effectively handle problem situations?

7. Is the salesperson open to and willing to try new ideas?

8. Are there personal problems that cause problems on the job?

Highly effective sales managers discuss these and other areas of assessment each time they are with the salesperson. They review not only the numbers from reports, but also the qualitative aspects necessary for success to support an over-all balanced assessment of salespeople's progress.

Casual as Well as Formal Assessment

Assessment happens in casual as well as more formal ways. After observing a salesperson's call on a prospect, the sales manager may offer a word of praise for something done well, pointing out how this will move the salesperson closer to a particular goal. At the end of a day or two of traveling together, the sales manager will sit down for a more formal coaching session. At periodic times of the year, the sales manager and salesperson will sit down for a performance appraisal. Sales managers continually let everyone on the team know how they are doing on their goals, praise progress, and get input on challenges that are causing goals to be missed. When appropriate, highly effective sales managers make adjustments to the activities and behaviors necessary to accomplish goals. Highly effective sales managers use the information derived from assessing to become better goal planners in the future.

Assessing Leads to Better Relationships

Assessing a salesperson's activities and behaviors can be an opportunity for very effective dialogue between the salesperson and the sales manager. Herb, my first Sales manager, used his assessment to merely tell me what was wrong and didn't tolerate any response. During field visits with me, Herb focused on what I did wrong. I cringed each time he announced that he was coming to visit me. During my annual performance reviews, there were many surprises, things that I wasn't aware of. Both experiences were negative.

Bert did the expected annual performance reviews in a mechanical fashion, following the company's prescribed process. Again, since there was no on-going dialogue about performance, there were often surprises. I felt that the annual review was a negative thing.

Phil talked only about the good things, so we never had an opportunity to determine areas that we might improve, or ways to improve them. Of course, I felt good after an annual review by Phil, or when he visited, but in retrospect, I didn't get an opportunity to discover areas that could be developed.

Nat realized that we all had a need to know how we were doing and he kept us continually informed. He seemed to know that we wanted to know if we were meeting his expectations. He knew that we weren't able to read minds, and unless he took the time to communicate his assessment, we would be in the dark. His assessments were focused on both strengths and areas that needed development. But when we discussed the areas that needed development, we did so in the context of action plans and timelines. That made me feel that he was interested and we were moving forward.

Assessment Can Be a Motivating Factor

Highly effective sales managers, who are interested in growing and developing their people, use assessing as a motivating factor. They introduce those areas they're assessing in a positive light, not in a critical way. As an example, they talk about strengths and opportunities for development, not things that the salesperson did right and wrong. They work with the salesperson to focus on how the strengths are contributing to successes, and how the developmental areas will make success even more attainable. They use the assessment process as an opportunity to talk not only about results, but also about activities, behaviors, skills, knowledge, and personal characteristics that drive results. Both the sales manager and the salesperson agree on individualized action plans that result in development. They agree on a timeframe for attaining these new goals. Assessments enable a sales manager to focus on his most important resource: his people.

Creating a Developmental Plan

Highly effective sales managers help their salespeople create a comprehensive plan to develop skills and competencies that help accomplish performance and career goals. One approach to accomplishing this would be to:

- Jointly review the current performance expectations and identify the skills necessary for the successful completion of these expectations.

- Determine the steps necessary to reach these goals.

- Identify the skills necessary to achieve these goals.

- Create a checklist of the identified skills.

- Create an action plan to improve this skill. This might include formal training or joint calls with the sales manager or with another team member that includes coaching to gain the needed experience.

- Create a written plan for follow-up along with dates, times, and responsibilities.

This collaborative assessing process enables the salesperson to take personal ownership for where he is today and where he wants to be in the future. It allows him to participate in short and long-term planning to grow. It helps to motivate him since he had an integral part in putting it together. And it reduces the anxiety of being assessed because it clearly defines goals and responsibilities.

Use the Coaching Process to Deliver Assessments

Highly effective sales managers are committed to growing and developing each salesperson and use assessment as an opportunity to understand strengths and areas for development. They understand how critical it is to align individual goals and expectations with the overall company goals and expectations. They provide candid discussion along with frequent and honest feedback. They focus on activities, behaviors, and results, showing the interdependence of all three. In the next chapter, we'll look at a method of coaching that creates dialogue and allows the sales manager to discuss both strengths and areas for development in ways that can motivate salespeople.

chapter five

Best Practice #4: Coach for Optimum Performance

Coaching is the most effective skill-development method sales managers can use. It should follow other methods of training and be related to them. That means that if you have a sales training program that your salespeople attend, your coaching should reinforce and support it. Use the same terms used in the training. Coaching's biggest advantage over classroom training is that it can be tailored to the individual, to his or her needs and strengths.

Options to Improve

There are two ways to improve: work harder or change the way we are doing things. Coaching is about changing by doing things differently.

Salespeople, like everyone else, have difficulty seeing how to do something different from the way they're currently doing it; they have blind spots. The power of coaching lies in discovering those blind spots and turning them into perspective.

Highly effective sales managers coach by looking at what the salespeople are doing now to determine what to change to make tomorrow better. Most salespeople are already working as hard as they know how; it's how they're working that is causing them the problem, not how much they're working. That means change is needed. The highly effective sales manager coaches his salespeople who are being defeated by their blind spots to do things differently. We'll talk more about the phrase "doing things differently" later in this chapter. The implication here is that those who are doing what they're doing today can become better if they do things differently the next time. That is a key principle of coaching.

The sales manager's challenge is to get people to see their blind spots. If you've ever worked with a salesperson who has been selling adequately for 20 years but not near his optimum potential, and you try to get that person to change, you're facing someone who doesn't want to look at his blind spots! Highly effective sales managers use coaching as a way to get people to see their blind spots and change.

The Value of Coaching

Coaching is getting to be a more familiar term in the corporate world although it has a long way to go to make the impact it has made in the sports and entertainment world. Coaches are often thought to only reside in the sports world or the world of entertainment, which they do. Why? Because professional sports and entertainment organizations know the value of a good coach.

Tiger Woods, the number one golfer in the world, used Butch Harmon as a coach. Butch could not compete with Tiger Woods in any PGA event; he doesn't have the natural talent that Tiger has, he doesn't have the experience on the tour, and he's in a different generation. In fact, as far as I know, Butch Harmon has never played on the PGA tour, and never won a PGA tournament. But Butch Harmon has helped Tiger to become the best at what Tiger wants to be.

The fact that Butch Harmon has not performed at the level that Tiger Woods has is an important point. Many sales managers feel that unless they have been top producers, and can sell as well as anyone on their team, they can't really coach someone, especially the superstars. As Butch Harmon shows, that is not true. Butch certainly cannot play golf as well as Tiger Woods. What is necessary is that the sales manager has an understanding of selling, demonstrates a coaching attitude, and follows a proven coaching methodology, which we'll discuss in this chapter.

The world of entertainment also uses coaches. Luciano Pavarotti was born with a wonderful voice, but he took (and probably still takes) lessons from a voice coach. I don't know who that voice coach is, but he probably doesn't have the natural talent that Pavarotti has, and he probably has not been as successful in opera as Pavarotti has. Again, the point is, it's not necessary that Pavarotti's coach be as good or as successful as he is. When Julia Roberts won her Academy Award for best actress in *Erin Brockovich*, after two previous nominations where she did not win, she attributed her win to Steven Soderbergh, her director (coach). Julia said[1], "I have an Academy Award now, and nobody else has brought that out. It's indescribable." Steven Soderbergh certainly can't play the parts that Julia Roberts can play, but he can help her play those parts to the best of her ability.

Why We Don't Coach

The point is that many people are born with exceptional talent, but it is through coaching that they reach the heights of their ability. Why, then, don't we see more coaching in the corporate world? When I ask this question in my seminars, I usually get the same three answers:

I don't have time. Coaching does take time. The interesting thing, it gives time back later on. In the beginning, when coaching is being implemented, it takes time for the manager to coach. However, as people become accustomed to being coached and realize the benefit to coaching, they tend to become self-coaches. When that happens, the time necessary for the sales manager to coach becomes available to do other things. In fact, that was one of the important points in the *One Minute Manager*: The Manager had time to do the strategic things necessary to run the business. His people had become self-coaches;

---

1 "What Oscar has wrought" by Claudia Puig, *USAToday*, March 27, 2001

creating one-minute goals, giving themselves one-minute praise and one-minute reprimands.

I don't know how. This is true also; most of us, unless we are involved in sports or the performing arts, haven't been exposed to coaching. And some of us who are involved in these areas don't have good coaching role models. The good news is that good coaching is a learnable skill, as we'll see in this chapter. It takes effort, like any other skill, that will result in becoming more effective at developing people. Long term, that's a good enough reason to learn how to coach.

I don't want to offend anyone or end up in a confrontation. This was certainly Phil's problem. Phil didn't want to offend anyone, and he certainly didn't like confrontation. Yet not dealing with issues that needed to be dealt with was costly to Phil and his team. Given the American management methodology of exception management, where the only time one gets any feedback is when they do something wrong, it's understandable why we would feel talking with someone about his performance could offend him. Yet, there are ways to be positive and point out performance issues that need to be done differently without offending. There are also ways to point out performance deficiencies without negative confrontation. We'll look at those methods in this chapter.

Two Important Coaching Points

Because most of us have not had any coaching role models, there are two important points about coaching that need mentioning:

• First, coaching is not an event. It is a process; it is on going. Coaches don't just have a coaching session once and everything happens the way they want from then on. Coaches have many sessions where they coach the same skill over and over, often focusing on the basics. Look at spring training for professional baseball players or pre-season training for professional football players. Here are professionals who have been playing the sport for most of their lives, and yet the focus at these training camps is on basics. It is this constant reinforcement that brings about improvement. Reinforcement shapes and builds desirable behavior. That means that as the salesperson slowly builds skills in some particular area, the sales manager continually reinforces by feeding back observations in a positive manner. Coaches don't just hold a one-hour session, cover all the important points, and then turn the individual loose to do his thing. Coaching takes time and repetition.

• Second, the most difficult thing about coaching is learning to put ourselves second. Coaches don't play the game; they watch. They let their players play. That is very hard for some top-performing sales managers to do. No matter how good the sales manager coach might be at sales, she has to put herself second to the salesperson. If you watch sports events, especially football or basketball, where are the coaches? They're not out on the field but on the sidelines watching everything that goes on. In fact, there may be several coaches on the sidelines watching and feeding information back to the players. And that brings up one of the most important skills that sales managers who coach utilize: feedback. As Ken Blanchard, in his book the *One Minute Manager* says, "Feedback is the breakfast of champions."

Feedback: The Critical Component

What is feedback? If you've ever flown on a commercial airline flight, you can credit your success in reaching your destination to feedback. As an East Coast to West Coast flight occurs it is not uncommon for the airplane to go off course about 90 percent of the time. But constant feedback to the pilot enables the airplane to reach its final destination. This same principle of feedback applies to salespeople. In order for salespeople to reach their goals, they need constant feedback on their performance from their sales manager. This ongoing feedback performs two functions: it helps keep the salesperson on track to achieve her goals, and it lets her know where she stands.

Feedback Guidelines

To be effective using feedback we need to be aware of some guidelines:

Feedback needs to be balanced. That means we give feedback about things the salesperson is doing well, and we give feedback about those things that need to be done differently next time. Notice the words I used in that last sentence: "well" and "done differently next time." Discussing what a salesperson is doing well is an effective way of encouraging and reinforcing those behaviors and activities the sales manager wants continued. Discussing what needs to be done differently is an effective way to encourage and reinforce change. If we only ever talk about things that went well, we will not be able to move people to do things that need to be done differently. And if we only ever talk about things that need to be done differently, people will get the impression that they aren't doing anything well. To be effective, we need to talk about both; to be balanced in our feedback.

Feedback needs to be given sooner rather than later. If you're on a call with a salesperson and you observe him doing something you either want continued or changed, give the feedback as soon as you can. Don't wait for a couple of days. When I ride with salespeople I give some feedback after each call. At the end of the day, we sit down and have an extended coaching session.

Feedback needs to be specific, not general. Focus feedback on things the salesperson said or did. Saying to a salesperson "good job" is a general statement and is not feedback as I'm defining it here. It is a compliment. I'm not saying we shouldn't compliment salespeople. What I'm saying is if we are to use feedback in order to encourage or discourage certain behaviors, we have to be specific about what those behaviors are. Saying to a salesperson, "I thought the graphic you used to show the advantage of tax deferral was really effective. It clearly showed how much more money she will have over the taxable products she is considering" is specific. Feedback needs to be specific, not general.

Explain why something is being done well, or why it needs to be done differently. We talked about making sure that we include "why" in the chapter on communicating expectations. When we're attempting to get someone to change, they want to know why. If we don't give the "why," the feedback is easily perceived as our opinion. "Why" helps to validate and justify. If we can't come up with a "why" then maybe what we're trying to get someone to do isn't important.

Don't use "but" between your comments about something done well and something you want done differently. Here's an example of how *not* to do it: "I liked the way you found out the prospect isn't the decision maker when you asked, 'Who besides yourself do you talk with regarding purchases like this?' But, you didn't ask if they had the money." "But" is an "eraser" word; it erases everything that precedes it in a sentence. "But" often comes across as criticism and when we use it in a sentence with praise, people tend to only hear the criticism.

Here's an example of feedback using these five guidelines. The Sales manager is talking with the salesperson after a call:

"I liked the way you said, 'Before I tell you about our widgets, may I ask you some questions to better understand how they would benefit you?' That clearly told the prospect what you wanted to do, and told him what he would get out of allowing you to ask questions.

"Next time I'd like to see you ask, 'Before we look at our line, who other than yourself do you usually bring in for a decision about widgets?' That will enable you to understand who the decision makers and influencers are in their organization."

- Notice the use of the word "I" in the example above. "I" messages are powerful, open, honest, direct messages. They make the user authentic, an important trait of successful leaders. They clearly communicate expectations. They show powerful praise.

• Notice how specific the feedback was. The sales manager used the salesperson's actual words. That makes the feedback very specific.

• Notice that the sales manager explained "why" what the salesperson said was especially well done. It "clearly told the prospect what you wanted to do, and told him what he would get out of allowing you to ask questions." Salespeople like to know "why."

• Notice the request by the sales manger for the salesperson to do something differently next time and the reason why the sales manager requests this be done.

The Impact of Coaching

In my seminars, I use an exercise called The Amazing Coach[2] to help people see the impact coaching can bring to another person and to set up the importance of feedback. I do this exercise before we discuss feedback. The Amazing Coach is "(An) exercise (that) is useful in two ways. The first is to give the sales representative an appreciation for the challenges their managers face in the coaching process. Second, it is a good opening exercise to use with representatives who will be acting as mentors to newly hired representatives."

The exercise is performed by dividing the group into two people teams. Each team consists of a coach and a sales representative. Everyone gets a copy of a maze, one of those things that have a place to start and a

---

2 Gary B. Connor, John A. Woods, *Sales Games and Activities for Trainers* (McGraw-Hill, 1997).

place that you want to end, and you draw a line through the maze from Start to End to show how to get there. The person on each two-person team who is going to be the coach also gets a copy of the maze answer key. The sales representative is then blindfolded after briefly looking at the maze. The coach stands behind the sales representative and tells her where to draw a line to go from outside the maze to the "Sale" in the middle. The exercise lasts three minutes and the winner gets a prize. As you can imagine when you have a bunch of competitive salespeople in a group, there is a lot of yelling and verbal guidance during this exercise.

After the exercise, we talk about how the coaches and the sales representatives felt during the game. The sales representatives bring up how frustrated they were because they couldn't see what the coach was telling them to do, how much pressure they felt because of the limited time and their coach's aggressive urging. The coaches bring up how frustrating it was because they couldn't get the sales representative to do what they told them to do. Most of them wanted to take over and do it themselves, a typical attitude of successful salespeople who have been promoted to sales manager. These comments help take us to a discussion of the two kinds of coaching: directive and non-directive.

Directive Coaching

In the Amazing Coach exercise, the "coaches" have the answer to successfully completing the maze in front of them; they know something the "sales representatives" don't know. Their job is to direct the sales representative to a successful conclusion quickly. How do they do that? They tell the sales representatives exactly what to do: "Move your hand to the left, continue going left, move to the right, etc." In directive coaching, the coach is presumed to be more experienced or have information that the person being coached doesn't have. Therefore, the coach tells the sales representative what the rep doesn't know.

We've all had directive coaching all our lives. When your Mother said to you, "Close your mouth when you chew," you were receiving directive coaching. The attitude of the coach is, "Because of my knowledge and experience, I can guide you."

Directive coaching has its place. New salespeople who have little or no experience respond well to directive coaching. Herb, from Chapter 1, is an example of a directive sales coach, and because I was new to selling, it worked well for a while. However, after a while, if all one gets is directive coaching, he is going to start to resent it. Remember the implications of Herb's methods: low morale, turnover, etc. Bert-like salespeople also respond well to directive coaching. It is important to them that they understand what the people in authority want and that they perform the way the sales manager wants it done.

Directive coaching is also important in critical or life-threatening situations. If your child was about to run out into the street and you saw a car coming, you would use directive coaching: "Stop!" You wouldn't say "tell me what we do before we cross the street," which is an example of the second kind of coaching: non-directive coaching. Directive coaching would also be used if a salesperson is giving wrong information that is critical to a sale. One way of handling that issue might be for the sales manager who is along on the call to say, "John, I have to apologize that I haven't gotten you the latest information on that feature. I just got it myself before I left the home office, and it has changed. The new feature is . . ." The sales manager tactfully corrects the salesperson without causing the salesperson to lose face or credibility.

Non-Directive Coaching

Non-directive coaching is a fundamentally different way of helping others compared to directive coaching. The attitude of the coach in non-directive coaching is, "I'll help you learn to help yourself." This is a powerful concept because it, in effect, teaches people how to coach themselves, which is ultimately what a sales manager wants to happen.

One of the ways non-directive coaches help others learn to help themselves is by asking questions instead of telling. This is often referred to as the Socratic Method. Socrates, the Greek philosopher who lived in Athens, Greece around 400 B.C. was a master of non-directive coaching. He taught by asking questions, making his followers think and come to conclusions on their own. His method drew the answers out of his disciples. When people come to their own conclusions they are much more convinced of the validity of the conclusion than when they're told.

Non-Directive Versus Directive

Non-directive coaches facilitate the learning process; they lead and make the learning easier. Directive coaches *give* people fish; non-directive coaches teach people *how to* fish. Giving people fish makes them dependent on the fish-giver, highly satisfying to the ego but very limiting if the fish-giver has many things to do!

If we were to compare non-directive coaching to directive coaching, we would learn that non-directive coaching:

- Takes longer. It is much quicker to tell someone something than it is to ask her questions that draw the answers from her. However, as I have said repeatedly, telling is very ineffective in developing people.

- Is more powerful. Directive coaches who seem to have the information have the power; when I can come to my own conclusions, I have the power. I can grow without the help of someone else. That's powerful.

- Is longer lasting in its effects. When I learn how to fish, I can fish for the rest of my life. When I have to get my fish from someone else, I have to go back often.

Most of us have not had the opportunity to work for a good non-directive coach. The people we have worked for have most often been directive coaches at best, or non-coaches. As I explained before, my first sales manager was a bark-the-orders-and-you'd-better-hop-to-it kind of manager. He was definitely a directive coach and as a new salesperson, that worked for a while. I didn't know any other kind until I met Nat, who was a non-directive coach.

Because of the power of non-directive coaching, we're going to focus on it in this chapter. Most people intuitively understand directive coaching, and have had experience with it. So, unless I make the distinction, I'm referring to non-directive coaching.

Below are examples that compare non-directive and directive coaching. As you can see from this abbreviated example, the non-directive approach makes the salesperson come up with his questions. There's nothing wrong with what the directive coach is suggesting, but they are the coach's questions. The salesperson will feel more confident using his questions. And through non-directive coaching, he has a process that he can use by himself in the future, to improve.

Ask More Than Tell

As the example also shows, non-directive coaches *ask* more than they *tell* and they often don't have the answers to the questions they're asking. We have to be willing to admit we don't know all the answers.

Non-directive coaching example	Directive coaching example
"John, let's talk about how you can uncover more prospect needs before you make your presentation. The more you know about his needs, the more specific you can make your presentation to this prospect. That can result in more sales for you. O.K?	"John, you're making your presentations before you have enough information from the prospect about his needs. If you're going to close more sales, you've got to uncover more needs before you make your presentation.
"What is an example of the way you ask the prospect's permission to explore his needs now?"	"After you get comfortable with the prospect, say, "I'd like to ask you some questions."
"How might you rephrase that question so that the prospect sees the benefit to him of allowing you to ask questions?"	"You can say that that will enable you to focus on the areas he feels are important."
"Share with me some of the questions you might ask to focus the prospect on the money he's going to need for retirement."	"Make sure your questions focus on the money he's going to need for retirement and how what he's doing today isn't going to be enough for him. Ask him, "If you continue with your current portfolio's performance, is it going to meet your needs when you retire?" "How quickly do you want your money to grow to your needed amount for retirement?" "How is what you're doing now working to get you to that amount?"
"How could you phrase what you're now asking so the prospect starts thinking about how what he's currently doing isn't going to work for him?	
"How could you phrase a question to get him to see the power of tax deferral over the taxable investments he's using today?"	"How much growth of your money do you lose each year to taxes?"

Focus on Growth of the Salesperson

Non-directive coaching deals with present issues with an eye on the growth of the salesperson. Asking questions that cause the salesperson to think and self-discover a solution is an example of dealing with present issues with an eye for future growth. For example, a sales manager observes a salesperson on several calls mishandling objections. Instead of empathizing with the prospect's stated objection, then asking questions to clarify the objection, the salesperson responds to objections by piling on features and benefits. At the end of the day of calls, the sales manager says, "Lets discuss the price objections we kept getting today. O.K.?"

Salesperson: "Sure. As you can see, everyone is really concerned about prices."

Sales manager: "Here's basically what I kept hearing today from the prospects: 'Your prices are too high.' Would you agree that that's what we heard?"

Salesperson: "Absolutely."

Sales manager: "I'd like you to try something with me to handle these objections. First, when someone says, 'Your price is too high' I'd like you to empathize with her. What might you say that would be empathetic to the statement, 'Your price is too high'?"

Salesperson: (Thinks for a few seconds, then says,) "Well, I could say, 'I can understand your concern about prices.' Is that what you mean?"

Sales manager: "Yes, saying, 'I can understand your concern about prices' is a statement of empathy. It doesn't mean that you agree with the prospect, it just means that you understand that price is a concern for this person. When people say that the price for something is too high, it can mean several things, can't it? It can mean it's higher than I want to pay; it can mean that it's higher than I expected; it can mean that it's higher than some competitor's price; it can mean that the prospect is using price as a way of not proceeding because he doesn't have the authority to make the decision. In fact, there may be many things it means. How can we find out which of these, or some other reason, might be the reason any particular prospect means?"

Salesperson: I guess I could ask, "Do you mean the price is too high compared to another quote you have?"

Sales manager: "That would be one way. How could you ask so that you don't have to guess at all the different possibilities? How could you ask so that the prospect tells you what he means?"

Salesperson: (Thinking for a few seconds, says,) "I could ask him what he means by the price being too high."

Sales manager: "Pretend that I'm the prospect and ask me."

Salesperson: "When you say, 'Your price is too high,' what do you mean by 'too high'?"

Sales manager: "Excellent. How will asking the question like that help you?" (And the coaching session goes on.)

How Questions Are Structured Is Important

As you can see from the example above, how questions are structured is important in coaching, just as it is in selling. Both open and closed questions are used in coaching, as the example above showed. By open questions, I mean those questions that cause people to think and share their thoughts, to participate openly in the dialogue. Open questions aren't always "questions." The statement, "Tell me your process for making prospect calls" is not a question but a statement; it requests information, which is what a question does. Other non-questions are, "Share with me . . ." or "Help me understand . . ." Good open questions get the salesperson involved and are especially useful in problem solving, which is what a lot of coaching is about.

Open questions usually start with "What" or "How." "Why" can be an effective start of an open question, although "why" can be challenging, so use it carefully. Watch your tone of voice and body language when asking "why" questions. Of course, there are the statements that expect an answer and those usually begin with, "Tell me," "Explain," "Share with me," and "Help me understand." It often takes some thought and practice to come up with effective open questions. Notice the open questions used in the non-directive coaching example above: "What might you say . . . ? Pretend I'm the prospect and ask me."

Closed questions usually get very short answers; they often start with verbs: "is," "are," "do," and "can." "Will you," and "where, when, would, and who" are also usually closed question words. One of the worst closed questions I hear often is: "Don't you think you should have done this or that?" It is clear from the way this question is phrased that it really isn't a question at all, but the speaker's opinion that he wants verified from the person he's asking.

Why Closed Questions Predominate

In my experience, I find that closed questions are the most often used questions salespeople use. Since open questions get so much more participation and more information, it puzzled me as to why salespeople don't use them more often. Then, one year at the beach, where my wife and I met with our children and grandchildren, I found out why people are so trained in using closed questions over open. Throughout the week at the beach, I observed my children dealing with their children, our grandchildren. The mother would say, "Do you want peanut butter and jelly for lunch or a hot dog?" Or, "Do you have to go potty?" Or, "Do you want to use the raft?" Over and over, the grand children, just like my children, were asked closed questions. Eureka, I had discovered why closed questions are used so much - Everyone is trained to use closed questions. That may not be the answer, but it certainly made sense to me.

A Coaching Method

We've looked at a lot of information about coaching, so let's look now at a coaching method. The method is outlined on page 113 in a worksheet that sales managers can use. Although the method might seem extended, it can be used in a very short period of time. Coaching can be a very quick process that happens as you walk out of a call and head for the second call, or it can be a more lengthy process. I once worked with bankers who prospected shoppers in the aisles of a supermarket. We'd finish one session with a shopper, and while we were walking over to the next aisle, we'd have a coaching session. Remember: **coaching is not a performance review**.

Below are some ideas on how to conduct a successful coaching session.

First, prepare for the coaching session. As in my supermarket example or in a curbside coaching session after a call, I had to prepare. Some points that helped that preparation include:

- Observe the salesperson. The most effective coaching happens when the coach actually sees and hears what the salesperson is doing. Remember the discussion about professional coaches in Chapter 3 of observing?

- Make notes either during the observation or afterward. I couldn't make physical notes in the supermarket, so I made some mental notes. What was I noting? A key skill or behavior or activity that needed either reinforcement or improvement. Again, coaching is not a performance review, so it focuses on very limited areas, not broad areas. An example might be focusing on asking open-ended questions as opposed to closed-ended questions. It doesn't focus on the entire sales call, just the parts that emphasize an area for reinforcement or improvement. Being too broad is more than most salespeople can handle, and the comments tend to be perceived as criticism, not coaching.

• Determine developmental areas to discuss. What is it that you want to continue to happen or what is it you want to change? That's what you want to focus on, and people change by small incremental steps.

Second, communicate your expectations for the meeting. Once you've planned and know what area you want to work on, you let the salesperson know.

• Explain what developmental areas you want to discuss. I might say something like, "John, I'd like to talk about the questions you used to determine that prospect's needs." Then I'd explain why I want to talk about this area and how the salesperson will benefit. Look at the next line:

• Explain how the salesperson will benefit from this discussion. I might continue, "Questions are the key to getting the information we need to focus our solution. Your questions can affect your close ratio." Then, I'd continue by making sure my salesperson is ready and willing to talk about this area. Look at the next line:

• Ask for the salesperson's reaction. I would say: "How does that sound to you?"

Third, obtain and offer input. Notice in this third step that "obtain" comes before "offer." This is really important in non-directive coaching, which is where we get the salesperson to do some self-discovery. People who self-discover some important thing are more likely to accept it than when they are told.

• Obtain input from the salesperson about areas that were performed well. Good developmental coaches start the session by getting the salesperson to focus on things that were performed well. How do you do that? I ask the question, "What questions did you feel especially good about that you asked while we were with that prospect?" Directing the salesperson to look at things he's doing well helps give some recognition and encouragement to the salesperson. That is very important when building a relationship with the sales team. Focusing on what went well also keeps the salesperson from beating himself up, which is what most want to do. He says something like, "I knew that I should have . . ." Asking for the salesperson's input on things done well keeps this negative atmosphere out of the coaching session.

• Offer your input about areas you thought were performed well. Here is an opportunity for the coach to do some reward and recognition through praise. Find something you can praise about the area you're discussing. This, too, is important for building a relationship and keeping the session positive. Too many of us want to jump in and tell a salesperson what she did wrong. "Right" and "wrong" are not words we use in coaching. What "went well" and "what would you do differently next time" are the key phrases to effective coaching.

• Obtain input from the salesperson about areas that need to be done differently next time. Once we have the salesperson's input on things that went well, we move the coaching session to areas for improvement. By asking the salesperson, "What would you do differently next time?" we shift, in a positive way, to developmental areas.

• Offer your input about areas you think need to be done differently next time. After the salesperson has had an opportunity to give you ideas about areas that need to be done differently, you give yours. Sometimes this is not necessary because the salesperson hits it right on the head. You merely need to ask, "If you do that differently next time, what will it mean to you?"

• Ask the salesperson to summarize what went well and what is to be done differently next time. Here's a critical point: the salesperson summarizes, not the sales manager. This assures that the salesperson heard what was said; it also helps keep the responsibility for what needs to be done in the salesperson's court, not the sales manager's.

• Cooperatively create an action plan and get the salesperson's commitment to the plan. Coaching sessions end with an action plan, developed by the salesperson, but aided by the sales manager if necessary. If there's no action plan, at best, the sales manager and the salesperson had an interesting conversation. Coaching is not about having interesting conversations.

• Thank the salesperson and end the session.

Fourth, follow up. Coaching sessions are reinforcement of what is being done well and encouragement for doing things differently next time, if necessary. There's only one way to know whether what was encouraged is being done, or what needs to be done differently is happening: that's through follow-up. Follow-up also sends a clear message about the sales manager's expectations: "I expect what we talked about to be done." How does the sales manager follow up?

• Observe again. Get with the salesperson soon and inspect what you expect. Is what you coached about happening? Is the salesperson continuing those things he or she does well that you discussed? Is the salesperson doing the things that needed to be done differently? Observing answers these questions.

• Assess improvements or challenges. Change is an incremental process, so where on the change continuum is this person?

• Coach again. Praise any movement forward, and reinforce the need to do things differently, when necessary. As I said before, coaching is not an event; it is an on-going process. Don't get discouraged that change isn't happening as quickly as you want.

Change takes time. Start the whole process over again if there are several areas that need coaching focus.

A Brief Method Recap

A brief recap of what we've just covered:

- First, the Sales manager observes the salesperson interacting with customers.

- Second, the Sales manager discusses her observations with the salesperson.

- Third, the Sales manager and the salesperson develop an action plan.

- Fourth, the Sales manager follows up on the action plan (inspect what you expect).

Who Should You Spend Time Coaching?

How do sales managers decide which salespeople to spend time with and coach? First, assess their results (their results versus their goals); second, observe them at work with a prospect, making prospect calls, etc. New salespeople usually require a greater time commitment from the sales manager than experienced salespeople. This initial time requirement will result in improving salesperson productivity and less of a time commitment in the future. From time to time any salesperson, no matter how experienced, may need extra assistance. But all salespeople, old, new, the best, and the poorest, should have a share of the sales manager's time.

Coaching When You Couldn't Observe

Coaching is best done after observing the salesperson during an actual call. However, that is not always possible, so the highly effective sales manager uses another method: the sales manager asks questions about a specific call the salesperson made. The questions are focused on obtaining examples of skills the salesperson used on the call. Here's an example:

Sales Manager:	"Betty, I want to talk about your call at Acme yesterday. That was one of the calls on your target list this week, and I'd like to get a sense for how it went. I'm especially interested in the questions you used during the call. How does that sound?"
Salesperson:	"That sounds great. I think we're going to get that order for 1000 widgets."
Sales Manager:	"That will certainly help you with your widget goal if we do. Why don't you share the question you asked to move from rapport building to investigating needs?"

Salesperson: "Well, after we spent a few minutes talking about his favorite pastime, which is fly fishing, I asked if I could ask some questions before I told him about us."

Sales Manager: "How did you phrase the question?"

Salesperson: "Hmmm, I said, 'In order to make sure I focus on your specific interests, may I ask you some questions before I talk about our widgets?"

Sales Manager: "I like that question. It shows the prospect that you're more interested in what he wants than in what you've got to sell. How did he respond to that?"

Salesperson: "He seemed pleased."

Sales Manager: "What were some of the questions you asked next?"

Salesperson: "I asked him how they use widgets today, what they have been paying for them, how often they order, things like that."

Sales Manager: "Share how you phrased those questions with me."

Salesperson: "'Do you use widgets today in your packaging area? Do you use more than 1000 per month? Do you order monthly, quarterly, semi-annually, or annually? Can you get shipment in 48 hours if you need them?' Those are the areas where we really shine. Those are my standard questions."

Sales Manager: "How might you phrase your first question so that you find out if they not only use widgets in packaging, but in other areas too, and how they use them?"

Salesperson: "How about, "Why don't you share with me where and how you use widgets at Acme?'"

Sales Manager: "What would it do for you if you started asking the question the way you just rephrased it, as opposed to the way you have been asking?"

Salesperson: "I can see that that would get the prospect thinking beyond just the packaging area, which is where I've been focusing. It would give me insight into a potentially larger order, also. That could get me a lot more business."

Sales Manager: "I agree. Let's talk about some of the other questions you're using also." (Coaching session continues)

Notice in the example above how the sales manager used questions to focus on areas. "How did you phrase the question?" was how the sales manager got to hear what actually happened on the call, although he wasn't there. Notice also how the sales manager worked to get the salesperson to understand and solve her problem with questions.

On page 113 is the coaching process in worksheet format. This can be used to cover the points of a coaching session. It is a good planning device. I often include ways I'll say something, so I don't forget.

If you haven't had a coach's attitude and have not done coaching, reviewing this chapter several times can help you. Consciously start practicing using these questions: "What went well?" and "What would you do differently next time?" Write out and use open questions that you can ask your salespeople when you're with them. Look for areas you can praise, and give praise often. Catch your people doing things right and let them know. Start asking for input before you give your input. Use the coaching worksheet on the next page. Coaching is a skill that can be learned when it is practiced.

In the next chapter, we'll look at holding people accountable.

Coaching Worksheet

SKILLS	✓	EXAMPLES FOR FEEDBACK

Explain what you want to discuss

Explain how salesperson benefits

Obtain and offer feedback

Ask salesperson what he/she did well

Coach gives areas he/she felt went well

Ask salesperson for next times

Coach gives his or her next times

Salesperson summarizes positives & next times

Create an action plan & get commitment

Thank salesperson and end session

Help development by following up on action plan

Observe

Assess

Coach

chapter six

Best practice #5: Hold Salespeople Accountable

Highly effective sales managers are accountable for making the sales team's goals; they accept that responsibility. Since sales managers cannot, by themselves, make the sales necessary to get the job done, they must rely on the sales team. That means sales managers must hold their people accountable.

Just as it is not an accident that defining and communicating expectations is at the beginning of the process, it is not an accident that holding people accountable is at the end. Highly effective sales managers first and continuously communicate what they expect and then hold their people accountable to what they communicate. Clear expectations and individual accountability to those expectations are the foundation of high performing sales teams. Highly effective sales managers communicate clear expectations and ensure individual accountability through the five best practices which systematically sets up a path for success.

• Define and clearly communicate expectations. Everyone is clear about expectations and is committed to them; the sales manager is clear that everyone is committed to these expectations.

• Observation proves that the expectations are being carried out, or deficiencies are identified when they aren't being carried out. Observation allows the sales manager to inspect what is expected.

• Assessment of goals that are good for the individual, the team, and the organization and that are agreed upon happens on a regular basis. Everyone knows what their goals are, why they are necessary, and how to accomplish them. They are committed to their goals.

• Coaching of individuals and the team happens on a regular basis to assure ongoing growth and development.

• Holding people accountable is not delegated but accepted by the sales manager as the only way to ensure that the process is intact.

Accountability: A Critical Link in the Chain

If any one of the five best practices is missing, the chain is broken and success will be jeopardized. Accountability is the final piece that is critical to the chain.

How do highly effective sales managers accomplish the necessary accountability?

- As the leader of the team, the sales manager keeps informed of significant opportunities, challenges, and obstacles as well as promised results, from herself or individuals on the sales team through weekly status meetings, joint calls, and monthly sales meetings. Keeping informed is necessary if commitments are to be made since commitments effect other divisions, the company, and stockholders.

- The weekly status meeting, joint calls, and monthly sales meetings enable the sales manager to make sure that the salespeople consider themselves stakeholders in what they're doing. Throughout each of the best practices the process emphasizes the importance of dialogue with salespeople individually. Each of the steps provides an opportunity for the salesperson to commit and become a stakeholder.

- The Sales manager doesn't accept excuses or justifications when results are not accomplished; she uses missed results as an opportunity to remind salespeople of their commitment and to hold them to it. Highly effective sales managers use these instances as opportunities to help their salespeople grow and develop. Growth and development is sometimes painful.

Although accountability opportunities happen each and every time the sales manager interacts with the salesperson, two different meetings enable highly effective sales managers to ensure accountability: the weekly status meeting and the monthly sales meeting. We'll look at both.

Weekly Status Meetings

In weekly status meetings, the sales manager and the salesperson discuss last week's actual activities and results, and next week's proposed activities and results. Goals and results agreed to for the previous week are discussed and commitments are made to new goals and action plans for the coming week. The purpose of the weekly status meeting is to:

1. Discuss last week's sales results and set goals for the coming week

2. Discover, establish, and reinforce best practices

3. Celebrate individual successes

4. Expose coaching opportunities

Weekly status meetings keep everyone focused on critical goals, allow salespeople to optimize their sales abilities, and produce accountability for results. The monthly sales meeting focuses on team accountability. Not only does the monthly sales meeting hold the team accountable, it also provides opportunities to:

• Generate team spirit, celebrate team successes

- Review results compared to the goal performance chart

- Develop skills during practice sessions

- Discover individual coaching needs

Let's look first at the weekly status meeting:

The weekly status meeting consists of two parts: first, a discussion by the salesperson regarding the results of his or her goal commitments from the previous week; second, a discussion of goals and action plans for the coming week. The meeting should take no longer than 15 or 20 minutes.

Weekly Status Meetings Train Sales People

The format of the weekly status meeting revolves around a set of questions the sales manager and salesperson can answer each week (See page 121). By using this set of questions each week, the salesperson becomes "trained" to have the answers prior to the meeting, allowing her to monitor her own success and keep the meetings short and informative. This consistency provides the sales manager with a diagnostic tool to assess performance and reinforce accountability. This process leads to long-term improved sales performance.

Weekly status meetings are conducted by the sales manager with each salesperson. When sales managers have salespeople in the field, away from headquarters, these weekly status meetings can be conducted by phone.

The Sales Manager's Role at Weekly Status Meetings

The sales manager's role during the meeting is to:

• Keep the meeting short, focused on the questions that inform about sales results and sales processes, and do not allow the salesperson to go off on tangents. During the salesperson's goal results report, the sales manager listens and asks questions to ensure understanding of what has happened, whether the salesperson is on-goal or not. To encourage each person to be candid, the sales manager should not show frustration or negativity to the report. Remaining neutral if the results are not good; positive and verbally recognizing good performance if the results are good is a way to encourage candor.

• Focus on goal setting, goal accomplishment, and key activities. (See questions below.)

• Recognize and praise successes. The weekly status meeting is an excellent opportunity to reward salespeople through recognition and praise. The sales manager can use feedback during these sessions. If the salesperson describes a certain question that she used in order to determine a need, the sales manager can praise this by saying, "I like that question. It is open and will get you a good insight into what the prospect is thinking. Good job."

• Listen for opportunities that indicate a need for individual coaching. Salespeople who are below goal and struggling with how to make goal may be candidates for joint calls and coaching opportunities. This meeting often brings these opportunities to the forefront.

- Discuss the activities planned to meet the new goals. The salesperson talks about the activities planned to make next week's goals. These might be prospecting opportunities in a certain industry, part of town, etc., or other activities such as seminar selling or trade shows.

Responsibility for Results

A productive weekly status meeting is one in which each salesperson takes responsibility for last week's results and commits to goals and activities to achieve this week's goals. Below are some questions for the sales manager to ask in these weekly status meetings:

1.   What were the results of your target goals for last week?

2.   What obstacles are you encountering?

3.   What plans do you have for overcoming these obstacles?

4.   What are you doing to improve those areas that are below your goals?

5.   What are your goals for next week?

6.   What activities have you planned to achieve those goals?

7.   What can I do to help?

The Salesperson's Role at Weekly Status Meetings

The salesperson's role during the Weekly Status Meeting is to:

- Report his or her results against the goals he or she committed to the previous week

- Discuss factors that affected results positively or negatively

- Commit to new goals and activities for the coming week

The weekly status meeting is a critical method for sales managers to keep informed and to learn which salespeople are focused on the selling effort in the most effective manner.

Monthly Sales Meetings

Where the weekly status meeting was with each salesperson individually and lasted 15 to 20 minutes in length, the monthly sales meeting is with the entire sales team and is 60 to 90 minutes in length. A good monthly sales meeting consists of four parts:

1. Review of the group's results for the month

2. Review of the group's goal performance

3. Reward and recognize successes for results, skills, and activities performed

4. Practice skill development

The Sales Manager's Role in Monthly Sales Meetings

The Sales manager's role during the meeting is to:

- Review the group's results from the previous month. This is a quick review of the entire group's result for the month and year-to-date. The weekly status meeting focused on last week and this week's individual goals and results. Now it is time to put all the efforts into focus by showing what the entire group accomplished last month and how that relates to the year-to-date goals. This review should take five or six minutes.

- Review the goal performance chart. Because goals are not always met as they are forecasted for each month and year, it is necessary to compare where the group is to where it needs to be. This is what the goal performance chart does. As an example, let's say that the group needed to sell 24 widgets this year, or two per month. It is the end of March, and you are reviewing the first quarter's results. The team sold 15 widgets already. That leaves nine to go to make your annual number, so you change the goal from two per month (what it was at the beginning of the year) to one per month for the remainder of the year. Using a goal performance chart allows the sales manager to see where the group is compared to where it needs to be, and make adjustments as necessary. This review should take 10 or 15 minutes.

- Provide continuing sales-focused training to salespeople in an upbeat, motivating, and exciting atmosphere. This is the crux of the monthly sales development meeting. Sales teams, like salespeople, have selling skill deficiencies to be developed that need constant honing. For the next 30 to 45 minutes the meeting focuses on specific selling skills such as overcoming objections, asking questions, building rapport, and whatever else the sales manager has seen that needs to be worked on. This portion of the meeting is when the five-step process outlined in Chapter 2, Communicate Expectations, should be used:

1. Explain what you want them to do and why it's important, both to them and to the organization.

2. Show them how to do it.

3. Allow them to try to do it.

4. Observe them as they try.

5. Praise success or any movement toward success. If they don't get it right, go back through steps two through five.

• Ensure salespeople understand and effectively use needs-based selling skills. By focusing on selling skills on a monthly basis, the sales manager ensures that each salesperson is aware of and can use the most effective selling skills. Proficiency will not come from these meetings, but these meetings ensure that all the necessary skills are communicated and that people have a chance to practice them. Additional coaching is often necessary to get to competency.

• Facilitate the meeting by asking questions that cause salespeople to think, to answer, and get involved. The monthly skill development meeting is not an opportunity for the sales manager to lecture. This meeting needs to be highly interactive if the sales manager is going to keep the interest of the sales team. That means involving the sales team actively throughout the meeting. Preparing for effective monthly sales meetings requires planning questions that cause salespeople to be involved. Salespeople like meetings that involve them and make them feel important. There are some excellent resources for holding these kinds of meetings listed in the Appendix.

• Make the meeting fun. The monthly sales meeting should be a "want to go to" kind of meeting, not a "have to go to" kind of meeting. That means to have some fun. The sales manager's overriding goal is to facilitate the meeting in such a way that the salespeople feel positive, productive, energetic, and excited to use the skills and knowledge they learn. Meetings should be fun because salespeople learn more and retain more of what they've learned when learning is fun.

• Stay on time. Begin on time and end on time. This commitment by the sales manager sends a strong message of the importance of planning and timeliness.

• Watch for coaching opportunities. Throughout this meeting, especially in the "allow them to try it" portion, the sales manager will see opportunities for follow-up coaching.

The Salesperson's Role in Monthly Sales Meetings

The salesperson's role in the monthly sales meeting is to:

- Enthusiastically applaud salespeople who are recognized

- Participate by asking and answering questions when necessary or appropriate

- Participate in the skill development practice sessions

Skill development sessions include sessions that reinforce salespeople's product knowledge from a sales-related point or reinforce their selling skills. Sales-related points about products include such things as the benefits of the product, target audience most likely to use the product, customer clues that indicate a need for the product, dealing with obstacles or concerns that might arise, competitive offerings and the "fine print" in those offers, etc. It includes an opportunity to practice.

Sales skill development sessions focus on activities and behaviors that ensure salespeople are using the best needs-based selling process possible. These sessions focus on how best to prospect, do pre-call planning, build trust and credibility, ask questions, make presentations, handle objections and concerns, ask for the business, and do post-call follow-up.

Monthly Sales Meetings Introduce Accountability

Monthly sales meetings are not only critical to the on-going skill development of a sales team but also introduce accountability through the goal performance review and the acquisition of effective skills. To be a success, the monthly sales meeting requires deciding in advance what you specifically hope to achieve and then carefully planning toward that goal.

At the beginning of the meeting, briefly explain what the meeting is going to cover and what you hope to achieve. Review agenda items and how they relate to your topic:

- "This month's sales meeting will focus on four things: the month-end numbers, the Y-T-D goal performance chart, awards for outstanding performance, and practice sessions. These sessions will help us feel more confident in using the skills to explore our customers' needs."

- "The agenda shows some discussion time. We want to focus this discussion time on opportunities and challenges for assessing customer needs."

Getting Participation

Getting participation improves the effectiveness of sales meetings. There are two ways to get participation: ask questions and have activities. The type of question that gets the most participation is the open-ended question such as:

- What is your reaction to that?

- What is your thinking about that?

- How do you see that playing out on the Acme account you're working on?

Some ways to wrap up a meeting are:

- Summarize and restate the main points of the meeting. Tell them what you told them. People usually remember the *last* things they hear. An example would be:

"We've talked about the importance of asking questions to determine prospects' needs. We said that that should start with asking permission to ask questions and stating the benefit for the prospect to answer our questions since this encourages the prospect to answer our questions. We also said that open questions get more information, and that to have effective open questions we need to plan them."

Letting *the group* summarize is an even more effective method for ending the meeting, especially if you want to find out what your salespeople heard!

Some important points for a successful monthly sales meeting that salespeople *want to go to* instead of have to go to include:

- Get participants involved all of the time. Get them talking and moving instead of just listening. The more actively they participate, the more they will remember.

- Make your *people* feel important.

- Tell them what you'll be doing, then do it and review it.

- Make follow-up clear with a handout and deadline request.

• Don't dominate the meeting! Encourage and develop interaction.

• Listen to salespeople's ideas and input. Ask questions. Don't argue. Don't digress.

• Treat salespeople as if they were customers *because they are!*

• Your overriding goal is to facilitate the meeting in such a way that the salespeople feel positive, productive, energetic, and anxious to use the skills and knowledge they learned.

• Focus on skills development.

• Meetings should be fun. Salespeople learn more and retain what they've learned when learning is fun.

• The way you handle sales meetings will be directly reflected in sales results down the road.

Sales managers get important information from weekly status meetings and monthly sales meetings. The information important for the sales managers to obtain during these meetings includes answers to the following questions:

1. What factors are contributing most to sales successes?

2. What is causing missed goals?

3. What steps are being taken to make up deficits?

4. What results are anticipated from those steps?

5.   Which activities are working and which ones aren't? Why?

6.   Who do I need to observe? When is a good time for this to happen?

7.   What coaching is needed and for whom? When?

8.   What competitive issues are being encountered? What is planned to deal with them?

9.   What obstacles are the salespeople having?

10. What training is needed?

11. What can I do to help my team?

The purpose of these questions is to understand where the group is in relation to goals, what activities are helping to achieve those goals, and what obstacles are causing goals to be missed. This information is the basis for determining observation and coaching sessions. These frequent meetings also clearly communicate what is important and what is to be done by each salesperson.

Debriefing Sessions

In addition to the meetings we've covered, there is another accountability session that highly effective sales managers conduct. I call it the debriefing session. The purpose of this session is to discuss a key sales opportunity and ensure an effective sales strategy for winning the business. In a debriefing session, the sales manager asks the salesperson a series of questions. Examples of the questions the Sales manager would ask include:

- "I want to talk about the Kazoodle account that you're working on. Tell me about the opportunity you've uncovered there."

- "Talk about the time, people, and money resources Kazoodle is willing to commit for this opportunity."

- "Who have you identified as the key decision makers, influencers, and others necessary to get this sale?"

- "Where are you in getting each of them on board?"

- "What objections or concerns have you uncovered and how are you handling them?"

- "What is the next step? How did you get agreement on it?"

The debriefing session is a powerful way to ensure accountability for an effective sales strategy for key accounts. It not only helps the sales manager keep informed, but also helps the salesperson think through important issues and how to plan for them.

Using the Web for Sales Meetings

In some organizations it is not possible to have a monthly sales meeting. When I was a National Sales Director for a Fortune 500 company located in Dallas, TX, my salespeople were in Los Angeles, San Francisco, Dallas, Chicago, Boston, and Washington, D.C. I couldn't have them in every month, so I planned quarterly meetings. The point is that some period more often than annually is important for team development. Today, there are options using the Internet to conduct meetings. One such service, WebEx, provides web conferencing, video conferencing, and online meeting services. You can find more information at their website www.webex.com.

conclusion

What does it take to be a sales manager? If experience is any indicator, the answer is to be a successful salesperson; that's the resume of most sales managers. But what does it take to be a highly effective sales manager? a successful salesperson that has a coach's attitude and implements the five best practices.

In today's highly competitive world, a sales manager can't just become effective; he or she must remain effective. Being a highly effective sales manager requires consistency and adherence to the five best practices. When sales managers think they can let up, they're in trouble. The five best practices that makes sales managers highly effective must become a part of their life; otherwise they fall behind. The question highly effective sales managers are asked is not, "What have you done?" but "What are you going to do for me today?" That's a fair question; it's the same question highly effective sales managers ask their salespeople.

The five best practices revolve around the basics; get them down and the rest will come. That's why they're called the "five best practices." There are many practices sales managers must master, but by consistently and systematically using the five best practices, constant improvement and steady performance will result. It doesn't come quickly but it will come, not with luck or good fortune, but through hard work using the process.

There's a story I love to tell at the end of my sessions that shows how highly effective sales managers develop their teams:

A man died and when he "came to" he realized he was not living. He looked around and saw an angel sitting by him.

"Would you like to take a tour?" the angel asked.

The angel led the man around. The first room they came to was darkened, with beautiful candlelight and many people sitting around a bubbling pot of delicious-smelling stew. Oh, what a smell! Just like mother's kitchen on a cold, rainy day.

"Where am I?" the man asked the angel.

"You're in hell," replied the angel.

"But how can I be in hell with such an amazing stew?" the man asked.

"Watch," said the angel.

The man looked again and noticed the people were severely emaciated, although they each had a six-foot-long spoon attached to their arms. As he continued to watch he saw that occasionally one person would maneuver the spoon into the pot, take out a spoonful of delicious-looking stew, and attempt to get the spoon into his mouth, only to watch the stew end up on the floor due to the length of the handle and the fact that he couldn't bend his arm.

The people were starving, with as much food as they needed just a spoonful away.

"What does heaven look like?" the man asked the angel.

The angel brought him to another room, which looked exactly the same as the first. The dim light, the people sitting around, the long spoons attached to their arms, the delicious stew. But there was a difference. These people were well fed and happy. There was laughter in the room. The man watched while the people took turns maneuvering their six-foot-long spoons into the stew, just as those in hell had done. But instead of trying to get the spoonful of stew into their own mouths, they were feeding each other. And all had food.

As this story shows, by serving their salespeople, highly effective sales managers serve themselves and their companies. Everyone gets their needs met.

appendix

Along with the many sales managers I have worked with, I have found the following resources helpful in my quest to learn to be a highly effective sales manager. I quoted from some of them in this book. I recommend all of them.

Sales Meeting Aids

Peggy Carlaw & Vasudha Kathleen Deming, *The Big Book of Sales Games* (McGraw-Hill, 1999)

Gary B. Connor & John A. Woods, *Sales Games and Activities for Trainers* (McGraw-Hill, 1997)

James Dance, *Get the Most Out of Sales Meetings* (NTC Learning Works, 1992)

Coaching

Ken Blanchard & Don Shula, *The Little Book of Coaching* (Harper Business, 2001)

V.R. Buzzotta, Ph.D., R.E. Lefton, Ph.D., Manuel Sherberg, *Effective Selling Through Psychology* (Ballinger Publishing Company, Cambridge, MA, 1982)

Marshall J. Cook, *Effective Coaching* (McGraw-Hill, 1999)

David Logan, Ph.D., & John King, *The Coaching Revolution* (Adams Media Corporation, 2001)

Nicholas Nigro, *The Everything Coaching and Mentoring Book* (Adams Media Corporation, Avon, MA, 2003)

Linda Richardson, *Sales Coaching* (McGraw-Hill, 1996)

Don Shula and Ken Blanchard, *Everyone's A Coach* (Zondervan Publishing House, 1995)

Chick Waddell, *Sales Coaching Playbook* (Winspirations, 1999)

Ron Zemke & Kristin Anderson, *Coaching Knock Your Socks Off Service* (AMACOM, 1997)

Sales Management

Ronald Brown, *From Selling to Managing* (AMACOM, 1990)

Robert J. Calvin, *Sales Management* (McGraw-Hill, 2001)

Joe Petrone, *Building the High-Performance Sales Force* (AMACOM, 1994)

Frank Pacetta, *Don't Fire Them, Fire Them Up* (Simon & Schuster, 1994)

Thomas L. Quick, *Making Your Sales Team #1* (AMACOM, 1992)

Neil Rackham and Richard Ruff, *Managing Major Sales* (Harper Business, 1991)

Bradford D. Smart Ph. D, *Selection Interviewing* (John Wiley & Sons, 1983)

Mark White, *Welcome to Sales Management* (AuthorHouse, Bloomington, Indiana,2004)

Selling

Sam Deep and Lyle Sussman, *Close the Deal* (Perseus Books, Cambridge, MA, 1999)

Todd Duncan, *High Trust Selling* (Thomas Nelson Publishers, Nashville, TN, 2002)

Keith M. Eades, *The New Solution Selling* (McGraw-Hill, 2004)

Robert L. Jolles, *Customer Centered Selling* (The Free Press, A Division of Simon & Schuster Inc., 1998)

Mahan Khalsa, *Let's Get Real or Let's Not Play* (White Water Press, 1999)

Sharon Drew Morgan, *Selling With Integrity* (Barrett-Koehler Publisher, Inc., 1997)

Neil Rackham, *Major Account Sales Strategy* (McGraw-Hill, 1989)

Neil Rackham, *SPIN Selling* (McGraw-Hill, 1988)

Neil Rackham, *The SPIN Selling Fieldbook* (McGraw-Hill, 1996)

Linda Richardson, *Stop Telling Start Selling* (McGraw-Hill, 1998)

David H. Sandler with John Hayes, Ph.D., *You Can't Teach a Kid To Ride A Bike At A Seminar* (A Dutton Book, Published by the Penguin Group, 1995)

Nancy J. Stephens with Bob Adams, *Customer Focused Selling* (Adams Media Corporation, 1998)

Jacques Werth and Nicholas E. Ruben, *High Probability Selling* (ABBA Publishing Co., 206 South Chancellor St., Newtown, PA 18940, 1996)

Other:

Ken Blanchard, Bill Hybels, and Phil Hodges, *Leadership by the Book* (William Morrow and Company, Inc. 1999)

Kenneth Blanchard, Ph.D., & Spencer Johnson, M.D., *Putting the One Minute Manager to Work* (William Morrow and Company, Inc., 1984)

Kenneth Blanchard, Ph.D. & Spencer Johnson, M.D., *The One Minute Manager* (William Morrow and Company, 1982)

Larry Bossidy & Ram Charan, *Execution, The Discipline of Getting Things Done*, (Crown Business, 2002)

Dr. Henry Cloud, Dr. John Townsend, *How People Grow* (Zondervan, 2001)

Jim Collins, *Good to Great* (Harper Business, 2001)

Terry Felber, *Am I Making Myself Clear?* (Thomas Nelson Publishers, 2002)

Dr. Thomas Gordon, *Leader Effectiveness Training* (Wyden Books, 1977)

Andrew Hill with John Wooden, *Be Quick – but Don't Hurry* (Simon & Schuster, 2001)

Lou Holtz, *Winning Everyday* (Harper Business Books, 1999)

Susan Scott, *Fierce Conversations* (Published by the Penguin Group, 2002)

index

D

F

G

about the author

For over forty years, Jerry Elmore has drawn from his own experiences in sales, sales management and sales training as well as the experiences of hundreds of sales people and sales executives of the Fortune 500 companies he has worked with. He has created and refined sales management leadership concepts that boost performance and improve teamwork. His approach has been embraced by sales managers who want to optimize the selling efforts of their salespeople to achieve the desired levels of sales volume, profits and growth necessary for a thriving organization.

Jerry is a highly effective sales management consultant and popular speaker with significant experience selling, managing and training sales managers and salespeople. Jerry lives in Midland, Georgia with his wife, Nina.

Printed in the United States
76317LV00003B/274